PHILOSOPHY AND RELIGIOUS BELIEF

Philosophy

———————

Editor
PROFESSOR S. KÖRNER
JUR.DR., PH.D., F.B.A.
Professor of Philosophy
University of Bristol and Yale University

PHILOSOPHY AND

RELIGIOUS BELIEF

Thomas McPherson

Professor of Philosophy
University College, Cardiff

HUTCHINSON UNIVERSITY LIBRARY
LONDON

HUTCHINSON & CO (*Publishers*) LTD
3 Fitzroy Square, London W1

London Melbourne Sydney Auckland
Wellington Johannesburg Cape Town
and agencies throughout the world

First published 1974

*This book has been set in Times type, printed in Great Britain
on smooth wove paper by The Camelot Press Ltd of
London and Southampton
and bound by Wm. Brendon of Tiptree, Essex*

ISBN 0 09 118750 8 (cased)
0 09 118751 6 (paper)

CONTENTS

PREFACE

Religious belief can take many forms and there are many questions that can be asked about it: this book is concerned with Christian religious belief and not with religious belief in general; and there are undoubtedly important aspects of Christian belief other than those discussed here and indeed other ways in which those that are discussed might be discussed.

The first chapter considers some basic questions about the nature of religious belief and related notions (like religious knowledge and religious commitment), and about ways in which religious belief or knowledge might be attained. The second chapter considers doubt and scepticism in relation to religion, and claims (a point further reinforced in the final chapter) that religious scepticism and agnosticism are not incompatible with religious understanding. The third chapter is about two views that attempt to assimilate religious belief to other sorts of belief, namely views that classify religious utterances under the headings either of moral utterances or of poetic utterances. Such assimilation can be but partial.

In the fourth chapter I discuss some elements in the defence and the criticism of theistic belief—the theistic 'proofs' of traditional natural theology, and the 'problem of evil' and Freudian views of religious belief. Although the so-called theistic proofs cannot be regarded as successfully proving the existence of God, neither, on the other side, is the problem of evil totally without answer, nor are Freudian views free from objection. Of course, that God exists is only one of the things that religious believers believe, and further-more the traditional theistic proofs constitute only one sort of consideration that might be offered in support of that belief by a believer. But the matters discussed in this chapter have generally

been agreed by philosophers of religion to be of particular importance. I suggest that the theistic 'proofs', although they may not
prove anything, are nevertheless of considerable significance for
the religious believer in another way.

The fifth chapter continues the study of Christian theistic belief
by examining a number of concepts belonging therein: miracle,
the soul, Christian virtue, sin, grace. The sixth chapter compares
religion with science, in the conviction that this is a useful way of
throwing further light on the nature of religious belief.

The final chapter deals with a question which has been not far
below the surface throughout, that of the *possibility* of offering
grounds (in particular, general grounds) for religious belief. This
chapter links in an obvious way with the fourth, but it is relevant
also to the themes of the first two chapters. A remark which occurs
in various forms throughout the book is that if religious belief is
belief—rather than (alleged) knowledge—then arguments in support
of it are not in any case essential. (Another recurring theme is that
if grounds for belief are under consideration then the philosophical
student of religious belief should be prepared to take note of psychological as well as logical grounds.) I argue in the final chapter against
views that hold that general grounds for religious belief are not
possible.

Chapters 1, 2, 3, 5 and 6, then, deal primarily with questions about
the nature of religious belief; Chapters 4 and 7 deal primarily with
questions about grounds or alleged grounds of religious belief.
There are reasons for the order in which the chapters appear, but
it may be useful to point out that they also associate themselves
together in this other way.

I have said something in various places about the question of
whether religious belief is *meaningful*; but I have not said very much
about it, partly because it has been a central topic of so many other
recent writings on the philosophy of religion, and partly because it
is a large and exceedingly difficult question.

I wish to express my gratitude to the following for valuable
critical comments on some of the chapters: Professor J. L. Evans,
Mr Vernon Pratt, Dr Robert Young. Chapter 5 incorporates (with
minor stylistic changes) most of my contribution to a symposium
on 'Christian Virtues', published in Supplementary Volume XXXVII
of the Proceedings of the Aristotelian Society; it is reprinted here
by courtesy of the Editor of the Aristotelian Society (© 1963 The
Aristotelian Society).

Cardiff   T. McP.

I

RELIGIOUS BELIEF

1. *Belief and practice in religion*

Religion has a number of elements, and an adequate account of religion is hardly to be got if any of these is totally ignored. In particular, there are two elements which have been given different emphasis from time to time, namely, religious belief and religious practice. Concentration on the belief element can undoubtedly lead to a one-sided picture of religion, and the belief element itself is not fully intelligible if separated from the practice element, as the latter is seen in participation in religious ritual or in the living of a life in accordance with certain moral policies. Nevertheless, the interest that philosophers have taken in religion has been chiefly in its belief element. I do not intend to break with this tradition, but, before going on in most of the rest of the book to discuss religious belief or knowledge, it is worth attempting in the first section of this chapter to put this kind of discussion in perspective.

There are several reasons why concentration on its belief element gives a one-sided picture of religion. The ordinary religious believer is probably not very reflective about his beliefs. He may be able to utter appropriate formulae, but he may not be able very well to explain these or defend them. Indeed, sometimes he is praised by religious leaders and teachers for the 'simplicity' of his faith, and it may be said by those who thus praise him that there is more of religious value in the acceptance of religious formulae, together with the attempt to live a particular sort of life, than in the kind of close examination of these formulae that is undertaken by some philosophers and theologians. The God of the philosophers has often been contrasted with the God of the ordinary religious believer, in ways intended to suggest that the latter is nearer the centre of religion.

Philosophy (even theology) is one thing; religion another. The philosopher's analytical or critical approach to religious belief may lead to a failure on his part to appreciate the role that it plays in the life of the ordinary religious believer; it is likely to miss the religious point of belief.

Something needs to be said on the other side, but let us now go on to note some other considerations which tend to suggest that too close a concentration on the belief element may be a mistake. The beginnings of serious interest in the 'essence' of religion—not of the Christian religion in particular but of religion in general—which coincided with the Romantic Movement at the beginning of the nineteenth century went along with, or was perhaps even the same thing as, development of interest in religious experience, in mysticism, in the psychological aspects of religion. Schleiermacher, and in the present century William James and Rudolf Otto, widely different as these writers are from one another, approach religion in a way that would have been largely inconceivable in any century before our own or the last. Although the expression 'religious experience' need not be understood purely in the sense of 'inner', 'emotional' experience, the tendency, and certainly the influence, of James' and Otto's approach is strongly in this direction. It is a familiar notion to anyone who has read Otto or writers influenced by him, that a proper under-standing of religion must accept it as being in the last analysis based upon a 'non-rational' or 'non-conceptualisable' foundation. This was not in itself new; but what was new was the presentation of such an approach to religion not as a preliminary to the traditional theologian's or philosopher's view of it as a collection of truth-claims to be expounded or explained or analysed, but as an explicit counter to that view, a kind of radical alternative to it. The whole idea of regarding religion as a human phenomenon is one that did not occur to more than a few people until the nineteenth century, any more than it occurred to them until then to undertake serious anthropological thinking and investigation. The notion of an 'essence' of religion—of religion as such, not this or that religion—is of comparatively recent growth. The assumption that there not only is such an essence but that it must lie in the 'psychological' realm, the realm of 'experience', was no doubt determined by a number of things. If such an inquiry were to be made for the first time today it would probably take a different form, sociological rather than (individually) psychological in character: the essence of religion is likely to be seen as lying in the role it plays in society, and not in the inner experiences of individuals. This kind of insight into religion is found in the nineteenth century itself—for example, in Marx and Engels—but the sociological approach to religion has not, until recently, had as much influence upon the thinking of theologians and philosophers of religion as has the Schleiermacher–Otto approach. (Sociologists would probably in fact repudiate an interest in religion 'as such', or in the 'essence' of religion: they are interested in religion in particular forms as these exist in particular societies.) At any rate, whatever one may think about the usefulness of inquiries into the 'essence' of religion, or of a search for 'the basis of all religion', in general the approach through religious experience both has been influential and offers a marked contrast to the traditional approach with its emphasis upon belief—or rather, upon the study of a set of propositions.

Alongside the growth of interest in the essence of all religion there went a developing and specific interest in the world religions—an interest in them not as instances of error but as subjects of serious study—and in primitive or undeveloped religions. Once embarked upon the comparative study of religion questions such as the following naturally arise. Could two religions have broadly similar moral policies but widely different belief elements? Answer: Yes; in the case of Christianity and Buddhism. Could two religions have the same kind of religious experience as their basis but have widely different belief elements? Answer: If Otto is right then this is the case with practically any two religions. These are questions about religion, in that they are questions about religions. A limitation of interest to the belief element of a single religion (Christianity), in the manner of most philosophers of religion, inhibits the raising of such questions; but a full understanding of any religion is probably more likely to be helped than hindered by a comparison of it with others.

Finally, we may return to a point already mentioned—a point that is, indeed, implied in all that has been said so far. Even if we are interested exclusively in one religion, it is still necessary that we consider questions about how within this religion—or how within a given society whose religion it is—the belief element is connected with the ritual element, the moral element, and the element of 'experience'; if we ignore these questions our understanding of the belief element itself will be incomplete.

So far I have been writing about the one-sidedness involved in too exclusive a concentration upon the belief element in religion. At the same time, perhaps not surprisingly, there is much to be said in favour of such concentration. Consider again the question of religious experience. Someone who has enjoyed what he would call a religious experience but who makes no attempt to describe this experience or to connect it in any way with his religious beliefs puts himself outside the possibility of discussion. We may note that he *says* he has had an experience, but if he will not say anything at all about the nature of this experience, or about whether or not it goes to confirm previously held beliefs, etc., there is little or nothing to discuss. Many will have something—even a little—to say about their experiences, for they will want to make them clearer to themselves, let alone to others. But now we see the importance of the belief element. The effect of religious experience is generally represented as being to confirm belief, or to induce it where it did not exist before. Even more fundamentally, we cannot give an account of an alleged religious experience unless we are able to say what it is an experience *of*. The precise form taken by religious experiences seems often to be determined by the expectations of the person having the experience; and these expectations are shaped by his previously held beliefs, or at any rate by the particular kind of religious teaching—in the shape largely of the imparting of propositions—that he has received: it has often been remarked that whereas both Protestants and Catholics may have visions, visions in particular of the Virgin Mary are much less likely to occur to the former than to the latter.

A similar point can be made in connection with the comparative study of religion. As it happens, this has commonly been an armchair subject, based on the reading of the sacred books of other religions, taken as sources for those religions' *beliefs*; so its practitioners are already concentrating on the belief element. But even if they had been more disposed to undertake anthropological field-work the belief element would still have been important. It is true that it is not possible fully to understand another religion unless one understands it from the point of view of its own adherents: what is important is what the sacred books, or the ritual practices, 'mean' to *them*. But this has generally been expressed in the form: 'They *believe* that . . .' (for instance, that there are evil spirits in the woods and that such-and-such practices ward off their influence; or that we pass through a series of rebirths, etc.). Both in the case of a claim to religious experience by a fellow-religionist and in the case of the study of other religions, once the question 'What does it mean?' has been put, on the commonest understanding of that question part of the answer has to be in terms of beliefs. The belief element in religion is then not just *an* element in it. No account of any religious experience, or any religious practice, however primitive the religion, will omit reference to beliefs, provided we suppose that the experience means something or that the practice serves some purpose. (We can, of course, refrain from asking questions like 'What does it mean?' or 'What purpose does it serve?' For the view that it may be inappropriate to talk at all of the 'beliefs' of another culture see Needham.)

One other point needs to be mentioned. This would, indeed, have been put in the forefront in the traditional kind of view—the view, say, of Aquinas. It has seemed important to many to define religious beliefs as clearly as they can, and to produce, in some cases at least, arguments in support of them. It is the belief element in religion that men are best able to *argue* about. The assumption that may be involved here—that religious belief is not 'rational' unless it can be argued for—can be questioned. It is not necessarily 'irrational' for a man to adopt a set of beliefs for which he is not prepared to give reasons. There is no obligation on a man always to back up his beliefs with reasons or arguments. We might find his failure to do so in a particular case irritating, and we might want to call him foolish or obstinate, etc.; but we should not have any right to call him irrational—unless, of course, in calling him irrational we merely wanted to point to the fact that he would not give reasons, but this would be a very weak sense of 'irrational'. Why should he give reasons if he does not want to, if all he is claiming is to 'believe' something? It would be otherwise if he were claiming *knowledge*. (Calling him 'irrational' would, for example, be justified if his beliefs themselves or his reasons for them were hopelessly internally inconsistent, or if some of his reasons were clearly irrelevant to the beliefs they were supposed to support, etc.) The view that it is 'irrational' to hold a belief that one cannot produce evidence for or give reasons for is one that is found among both supporters and opponents of religion. A general assumption to the effect that it is *never* justifiable (logically? morally?) to believe *anything* without evidence, or on insufficient evidence, has sometimes been made. Yet there seems no good reason to assent to this. Unless, that is, 'belief' is taken as equivalent to 'knowledge'. Generally, a man may believe anything he pleases; but if, when he claims to believe, what he really means to say is that he knows, *then* we would usually be justified in saying that he cannot be allowed to 'believe' (=know) what he pleases. (There are, no doubt, knowledge-claims which do not need support by arguments or reasons; but our concern here is with the broad contrast between cases where arguments or reasons can properly be demanded—knowledge—and cases where they cannot—belief.) It is worth remarking that traditional natural theology gives a centrality to sharp definition of religious concepts and to argument in support of religious doctrines which would simply be denied by many religious thinkers since Kant and Kierkegaard.

The expression 'religious belief' is commonly used, as it is in the title of this book, as a blanket term, to cover not only religious belief in a narrower sense (where belief can be contrasted with knowledge) but also religious knowledge (or claims thereto), religious commitment, religious faith, etc. The kind of analysis that it would be appropriate to give of religious belief is in various respects different from that which it would be appropriate to give of religious knowledge. The degree of ambiguity that there is in the expression 'religious belief', it is possible to suppose, might offer the religious believer an all-too-easy way of escape from criticism. He might begin by defending a certain position, but if criticism of its presumed rational foundation becomes too destructive might retreat into an admission that the position is after all only one that he 'believes' and that therefore does not *need* to be supported by argument: he might, that is, decline from an implied claim to know *p*, perhaps through an amendment of this to a claim merely to strongly believe *p*, to the position of one who just 'happens to believe' *p*. At all of these stages, as far as its verbal expression is concerned, his claim can be put in the form, 'I believe *p*'.

2. *Kinds of belief*

Religious believers claim to *believe* or to *know* something, or to possess *understanding* or *faith*, or to be *committed* to something. Several lines of inquiry offer themselves. What is it that is the object or objects of such claims? What kind of knowledge, belief, understanding, faith, commitment, etc., is claimed? How far is belief, etc., in a religious context similar to or different from belief, etc., elsewhere? Are there kinds of belief, etc., found only in religion and not elsewhere? How is religious belief or knowledge got—that is, by what methods or techniques? Let us take religious belief as the central concept and make reference to the others as may be necessary. I now proceed to take up some of these lines of inquiry.

The object of religious belief is sometimes a proposition ('I believe that Jesus Christ is Son of God'), sometimes a person ('I believe in God'). Similarly, the object of faith is sometimes a proposition (or a number of propositions, which taken together make up a statement of the Christian faith), sometimes a person (Jesus, or God). Similarly, again, in the case of commitment. Let us use the term 'propositional belief' for the kind of belief exemplified by 'Jesus Christ is Son of God', and the term 'personal belief' for the kind exemplified by belief in God. The expression 'personal belief' may seem to beg certain questions. Is God a person? May not something other than persons be the object of this kind of belief? (For example: a man may say, 'I believe in democracy'.) But the expression 'personal belief' is intended here merely as a convenient label, and no assumptions are being made about the answers to such questions as these. (For a valuable discussion of these two kinds of belief see Price, pp. 426–54, reprinted in Mitchell [3].)[1]

What is the relation between the two types of object? In particular, it might be wondered whether the difference between, say, 'I believe that God exists' and 'I believe in God' is any more than verbal. But the difference surely is more than verbal. For someone to say that he believes in God is for him to say more than that he believes in the existence of God; it carries an implication of trust, or commitment. I believe that the Dalai Lama exists; but I do not believe *in* him, as the Christian believer would say he believes in God. I am not a follower of the Dalai Lama; I do not trust in his leadership or his wisdom; I am not committed to him.

The beliefs of an adherent of a political party may also be partly propositional and partly personal. It is difficult to think of any third sphere of belief which shares this characteristic with religion and politics. No amount of dramatisation of the personalities of great scientific discoverers or great historians (or the historical personages about whom they write) will alter the fact that in these fields belief is propositional. The case of philosophy is perhaps a halfway house: neither Socrates nor Wittgenstein (to take one ancient and one modern example) regarded philosophy as merely a body of propositional knowledge, and they are both men who may be said to have had disciples. However, religion and politics are the only really unequivocal cases where the two sorts of objects of belief are normally present together.

It might appear that religion is a stronger example of this than politics, in the sense that while a man's religious adherence might be said to involve him inescapably in both propositional and personal beliefs, his political adherence can much more easily be limited to propositional beliefs. But this is probably a matter of cultural context. In our society, a man may adhere to the Christian religion and to the Conservative party, and in the case of the former adherence there will probably be personal belief, and in the case of the latter there probably will not. But in some other societies political adherence may involve a large element of personal belief, perhaps a much greater amount of personal belief than of propositional (e.g. Ghana under Nkrumah). And in the case of religions other than Christianity, the element of personal belief may be slight, or non-existent (e.g. some kinds of Hinduism). The point is not that it is essential to religion or politics that they always contain a measure of personal belief; but rather that it is never inappropriate to say of an instance of religious or political belief that it is partly personal,

[1] References, throughout, are to the Bibliography, pp. 125–6

whereas it would be inappropriate to scientific or historical beliefs (in any culture) that they should be partly personal.

Propositional belief may seem to offer the philosopher more scope for investigation than does personal belief. Not only is the quantity of material greater; but also there are a number of different types of question that can be raised about that material: the philosopher can concern himself with the content of the propositions, with the relations of implication, if any, between certain of them, with their character as literal or non-literal, with the grounds on which it would be reasonable to hold them; and so on. By contrast there may seem to be little for a philosopher to say about personal belief. It may be the case that techniques applicable in the examination of propositional belief are not appropriate for the study of personal belief. At the same time, it would surely be wrong to let capacity for responding to particular investigatory techniques be the test for what is important in any field. There is a reciprocal relationship in this matter. The invention of new techniques of investigation can virtually create a new branch of study. In general, the concepts we bring to our experience can help to determine where we draw the boundaries between one field of study and another, and certainly play some part in the determination of what is 'important' and what is not. The study of personal belief has not been much undertaken by philosophers (but, again, see Price); but it would seem to be a necessary study if religious belief is under consideration.

The interest of the philosopher of religion in the *content* of religious propositional belief is partly an interest in arriving at a delimitation of the field of religious propositional belief. What are religious propositional beliefs, as opposed to the propositional beliefs of economists, physicists, etc.? They are beliefs about God or about Jesus of a kind authorised by the Bible or by the tradition of the Church or certain branches of the Church, the teachings of Jesus as recorded in the Bible or as interpreted by the Church or by certain individuals. To say this is, however, hardly yet to have stated the content of Christian religious belief, but rather to have mentioned certain formal features of it. As far as the content is concerned, the philosopher generally limits himself to discussing certain examples, such as: 'God exists', 'God loves us', 'We shall survive bodily death'. It would be inappropriate for a philosopher—though not for a theologian—to become too closely involved in the details of the content of the Christian faith. At the same time, although examples might, presumably, be chosen at random (given that the subject matter can be independently delimited in some such way as that just mentioned), they are in fact not chosen at random. Indeed, to refer, as I have, to the propositions chosen for study by philoso-

phers as 'examples' does them less than justice; for it suggests that
they might be replaced by other propositions without serious loss.
But this is misleading. The propositions typically taken for discussion
by philosophers belong in a tradition of discussion; and, as is usual
in such matters, the tradition is to a large extent a self-perpetuating
one. The propositions in question are apt to strike the philosopher
as particularly worth discussing partly for the reason that they have
been already, through a long past, a good deal discussed. There is
also the further point that they have been presented by, and discussed
by, acknowledged authorities—the founders of religions, its prophets,
or its great theologians. But the discussion would probably be justified by those who engage in it on the grounds that the propositions
they discuss are in their subject matter important. And, certainly,
matters of life and love and death, of eternal salvation or damnation,
and the like, are matters of importance.

It has sometimes been supposed that the religious believer has
a source of belief not open to others, or that he has a special method
or technique of discovery not available to others. There are several
more specific questions here.

First, the question of a source. The Bible has been thought of
as such a source, or the teachings of the Church. The source is
commonly claimed to be authoritative; and the concept that needs
to be pursued is that of authority—a concept of central significance
in religion, or at any rate in traditional religion, which, indeed, is
partly defined in terms of authority. Revelation has also been
regarded as an authoritative source of knowledge. But 'revelation'
is ambiguous as between the contents of revelation and the process
or act of revelation. Furthermore, within the former it is possible
to distinguish between the Bible, or another such book, as *containing*
revelation, and the 'truths' revealed to an individual by 'direct
revelation' from God. And as far as the Bible itself is concerned it
is possible to distinguish still further, to adopt the formula devised
by William Temple, between revealed truth and truths of revelation.
(The distinction—in concrete terms—is between the view of the Bible
as a book literally or almost literally dictated by God and the view
of it as a book containing indications of truths about God.) We
need to note further that the source of religious knowledge might lie
not in authoritative documents or the like but in a personal authority.
If a prophet, reformer, etc., is regarded as having authority, then
this makes him an authoritative source of the religious beliefs of
others—that is, of some of them, for his authority itself will generally
derive from a set of existing beliefs or from an existing religion.
'For he taught them as one having authority, and not as the scribes.'

Secondly, let us turn to the question of methods or techniques.

There are accepted techniques for the cultivation of mystical experience, and it has been claimed—perhaps particularly by its
critics—that mystical experience provides *knowledge* of God that
cannot be got in any other way. And prayer has been held to lead to
a closeness to God that is not to be attained without it. In general,
it is often said that a religion is fully intelligible only from the inside,
so that those who are not themselves religiously committed in a
particular way can never understand what is understood by those
who are so committed. This raises a wider question than one about
special techniques of religious understanding or discovery, for views
of the kind mentioned in the preceding sentence need not include
reference to such techniques, and, indeed, may deny that there are
special techniques in this field (see Chapter 7).

However, questions do arise about the possibility of a special
religious way of coming to know or believe; and this line of inquiry
I shall pursue further in the remainder of the present chapter.

3. *Special techniques?*

Are there special techniques or methods open to the religious
believer that are not available to others? The short answer would
seem to be yes. There are techniques of prayer, as has just been
remarked, and books to explain these techniques to those who want
to know how to pray properly. Fasting can be regarded as a method
for creating the right conditions for prayer. Some of the Christian
mystical writers have made a particular point of explaining methods
or techniques of contemplation. What is experienced in contemplation may sometimes be said to be ineffable, but the methods by
which it can be attained have on occasion been outlined in a fairly
practical way.

How far is what is attained through the techniques of the mystic
to be called knowledge or belief? It seems to be a mistake to suppose
that mystics aim at acquiring or communicating knowledge-that or
belief-that, to suppose that what they are doing is attempting to
convey information, in particular information about God. It may
be that they are trying to point to an experience, but not altogether
to articulate it and not at all to give information about God. The
words they write might indeed be seen as themselves part of an
experience rather than as an attempt to explain, or even state, an
experience. A poet, somewhat similarly, need not be seen as trying
to explain something or to give information; not even information
about his own state of mind. The poem *is* his 'experience': it is not
a set of propositions in which he attempts to say what his experience
is. Ambiguities can arise in cases where it is assumed something is
intended literally; information can fail to be conveyed in cases where

it is reasonable to suppose the intention is to convey information. But both these assumptions can be questioned in the case of mystical utterances. Some criticisms of mysticism (e.g. those of Sir Alfred Ayer) seem to be based on the latter assumption (see Ayer, pp. 118–19).

If mystical techniques *are* to be regarded as ways of acquiring propositional knowledge or true propositional belief then, if they are to deserve to survive, they must at least produce results that are unambiguous and that provide clear information. If what they produce is unclear they would seem to be inadequate techniques. For knowledge about God we should need to look elsewhere; to the traditional theistic proofs, perhaps. It will not do to say that mystical techniques do provide knowledge about God despite the fact that what they offer is obscurity and ambiguity. Propositional 'knowledge' that is *fundamentally* obscure or ambiguous is not knowledge at all. Either what is produced by mystical techniques is not really, but only apparently, obscure and ambiguous, or it is a mistake to regard mystical techniques as techniques for obtaining propositional knowledge. (They might nevertheless, of course, be regarded as a basis for personal belief, or faith, etc.)

If mystical techniques are not techniques for the obtaining of propositional knowledge what might they be? A possible analogy would be with techniques for the improvement of physical health or strength, which might be seen as an end in itself or as a means to a longer or happier life. The weight-lifter, or the health food addict, may be strongly interested in the theory of weight lifting or the theory of diet, but the techniques he uses, though he may adopt them on the basis of certain theories, are not intended to deepen his understanding of such theories; they are intended to achieve a certain practical end (health or strength) which is other than either the techniques or the theories—an end which the techniques are techniques for achieving and which the theories are theories about. The end in view here is not naturally to be described by the words 'knowledge' or 'belief': it is a certain condition or state or quality of life. The situation of the mystic seems to resemble this at least as much as it resembles that of the seeker after knowledge-that. (There is a sense of 'knowledge' where it does refer to something like a quality or condition of life, where 'wisdom' is a possible synonym. The wise man is not just the man who possesses a great deal of knowledge-that; indeed, he may not be particularly well-informed; what he has is experience, judgement, etc. But this is not the sense of 'knowledge' that I have in mind in the foregoing, nor is it the sense that the kind of critic that I have exemplified by Ayer has in mind.)

The idea that there is a special religious way of obtaining propositional knowledge is one that arises when a particular model—that
of techniques of discovery—is assumed in accounts of the practices
of mystics. But the other model—that of techniques of body building
and the like—is a better one. First, it is better on account of the point
made above about the ambiguity and obscurity of mystical utterances,
acknowledged alike by many supporters of mysticism and by many
critics of it, which suggests that information is not in any case the
aim; for a technique for getting information that produced con-
sistently unclear results would surely have been abandoned long
ago. (There is, of course, the further possibility that the subject
matter—God—is inherently beyond our clear understanding. I
shall not go into this possibility here.) And it is a better one, secondly,
on account of the attitude of Christian mystics themselves, who have
commonly aimed at oneness with God rather than at information
about God. (There are, of course, different kinds of mystics, and
this is not meant as an account of all mystics.) On the weight-
lifting model, the notion of there being a special religious way of
obtaining propositional knowledge does not even arise, whether for
criticism or for defence. If we are to speak of knowledge in the context
of mysticism, it is personal knowledge, parallel to personal belief,
that we probably ought to have in mind. But 'knowledge' is in any
case a somewhat misleading term to use here, in that it tends most
naturally to suggest 'knowledge-that'. The mystic 'has' or 'enjoys'
his mystical experiences, and any terminology that suggests he
embarks upon mystical practices primarily in order to acquire
information, or that he would think it right to speak in terms of the
information he now possesses through his mystical experiences,
seems foreign to what mystics themselves have understood by mysticism.

I have been concerned to suggest that what are sometimes supposed to be special techniques for the acquiring of religious propositional knowledge may not be techniques for the acquiring of
propositional knowledge at all. If this is correct, then it might seem
not to be necessary for us to take these techniques into account in
our discussion of religious belief. In any case, it is often maintained
that the sources of a claim to knowledge are irrelevant to our
assessment of the truth of what is claimed; it is said that what matters
is whether a proposition is true, not how we have come by it: and if
this is so it might seem that we could safely leave aside all questions
about the methods of mystics.

However, this is a position that cannot be accepted without
qualification. The origins of a belief are sometimes relevant to our
assessment of its truth; for instance, if we thought there was good

reason to suppose someone's belief to be 'wishful thinking' (see Chapter 4, section 5), or if someone were to assert something on the authority of another person notorious as a liar. Beliefs are not held in a cultural vacuum; and not only is it the case that what people believe cannot be isolated from what sort of people they are and what sort of influences there have been upon them, but neither can questions of truth always be so isolated. It is natural to want to say that from biographical or psychological facts about individuals nothing follows that can have a logical bearing upon, for example, questions about the existence or nature of God. But religion is a way of life and not just a set of beliefs; and religious beliefs are neither fully intelligible nor easily to be labelled 'true' or 'false' in isolation from religion in all its aspects. And religious experiences are of *religious* significance and not 'merely' biographical or psychological significance. Indeed, that Christian mystical experiences are of Christian religious significance can hardly be denied, and it may well then seem over-intellectual to deny them some logical relevance to religious belief; for it is a particular application of the general assertion that beliefs are not held in a cultural vacuum that religious beliefs are not held in a religious vacuum. At an elementary level, in order even to recognise an experience as an experience of God, we should need the concept of God. We have referred already to the fact that Protestants rarely have visions of the Virgin Mary. It is not possible to separate Christian mystical experience from their background of religious teaching and tradition. Could a Martian have experiences which he could recognise, purely from the experiences themselves, to be genuine Christian religious experiences? There is an absurdity in the idea. Christian religious experiences occur against a background of Christianity. Mystical experiences are sometimes said to be purely 'private', incommunicable and self-authenticating. But they are not in fact incommunicable: mystics have written books, although perhaps only other mystics can hope to understand them very well. And they can hardly be totally 'private' or self-authenticating if they are *classifiable*—even merely classifiable as mystical experiences, let alone as Christian mystical experiences or in more detailed ways still. It may well be that someone who enjoys a religious experience considers that the experience bears upon itself the marks of its own authenticity; but this will be because he is bringing to it certain expectations, which he finds fulfilled. He may not spell out those expectations either to himself or to others, but he could do so; and, indeed, they need to be spelled out if a complete account is to be given. An experience may well appear to be purely self-authenticating if a necessary background is taken for granted and not made explicit. At least some criteria for the truth or falsehood of religious doctrines come from within religion (whether criteria come *only* from within we shall consider in the final chapter), but to say that they come from within religion is to acknowledge that religious mystical experience (which itself is not separable from a religious background) may have its own contribution to make to the establishing of criteria in the case of doctrines. A doctrine—for example, the doctrine that God loves us— may be 'confirmed' through mystical experience; the mystic may through experience become convinced of its truth as he was not previously: whether this doctrine is true or not is not to be established without reference to the total religious context. To say this is not to agree with the critics who suppose mystical practices are simply (rather inefficient) ways of acquiring information or knowledge-that.

4. *Commitment*

In the final section of this chapter I consider more closely the question of authoritative sources of knowledge. It will be convenient to treat religious commitment as the central idea in this section.

The notion that there can be authoritative sources of knowledge in any field is one which has come under attack from Sir Karl Popper and others following him (see Popper, pp. 3–30). Among these followers, Dr W. W. Bartley has developed Popper's ideas with particular reference to religion (see Bartley). Bartley maintains as a general position that any view that rests upon a claim to have found an authoritative source of knowledge has a basis that is ultimately irrational; and that this is a fatal weakness if its holders are to be able to criticise rival positions. Suppose, for example, that an empiricist were to criticise religious belief on the grounds that it is irrational—which from his point of view would mean that it is not capable of empirical verification. The religious believer might properly retort that the empiricist's own position is ultimately just as irrational; for it is based upon a principle (that the test for truth in propositions is conformity to sense experience) to which the empiricist is committed but which in the nature of the case he is unable to defend in the way in which he maintains that all claims to knowledge must be defended (there cannot be empirical evidence for empiricism). The fault would lie, according to Bartley, in the empiricist's claim to have, in empiricism, an authoritative source of knowledge. (We need not consider whether Bartley is right in his interpretation of empiricism.) Unless he gives up that claim he can hardly expect to be listened to with respect when he criticises some other position as 'irrational' in the sense that it does not conform to the (his) test for rationality; that test itself has an irrational basis. What is needed is the abandonment of any claim to an authoritative source of knowledge and its replacement by the adoption of *critical methods*; provided, of course, that a thinker does not merely replace commitment to an ultimate principle by commitment to critical methods: the critical methods are to be used as they seem useful, and there is to be no question of final commitment to them

Bartley's argument seems to me to raise several difficulties. Commitment to an ultimate first principle or to an authoritative source of knowledge may well seem 'irrational' in the sense that the rational man is often thought of as the open-minded man, the man who does not claim (or at any rate, does not claim too soon: an important amendment) to have found the final solution to a problem. But what is needed here is something that Bartley does not provide: some closer examination of *kinds* of commitment. It may be that there are some kinds of commitment that deserve to be ruled out, but others that do not. Further, it may be that although commitment, of a certain kind, is indeed 'irrational', that kind of commitment is still in some cases necessary: a thing can be both objectionable and unavoidable.

As far as variety of kinds of commitment is concerned, we may note the following. Far from commitment as such being irrational, we are prepared to distinguish between rational and irrational commitment, or at any rate between degrees of rationality in commitment. There is a difference between the man who adheres to some position simply because, let us say, he supposes he must adhere to something but can give no good reason why he adheres to it, and the man who has thought about some matter and thinks it important to give reasons as far as he can for the position to which he is committed.

Not only can there be degrees of rationality in commitment, in the sense that some cases of commitment have a firmer rational basis than others, there are also differences of degree in the strength with which a commitment, however based, is held. There is strong commitment and weak commitment. Some men are prepared to give their lives for what they believe in; others decidedly are not, yet might still claim to be committed. It is possible, of course, to say that weak, or at any rate very weak, commitment is not commitment at all; that the test for whether a man is really committed is whether (say) he is prepared to die in the cause of democracy, or prepared to forsake father and mother to follow Christ. But it is unrealistic to set the standard as high as that. It is of the nature of democracy that men's commitment to it may be fairly weak; part of the ethos of democracy is that fanaticism is frowned upon. And modern Western Christianity, whether Protestant or Catholic, is generally adhered to in a fairly conventional and 'unenthusiastic' way. It would be possible to say, in face of this situation, either that present-day liberal democracies or present-day Christianity exhibit few instances of committed men, or that the kind of commitment that they attract is relatively weak. The latter alternative seems to me preferable. That commitment needs to be intense to deserve the name at all does not seem obviously true.

Commitment can be deliberate or it can be involuntary. It can be unwelcome, as when a man finds that he is committed to a certain position that he never intended to commit himself to but which has been shown to him to follow logically from some other position to which he is committed. Incidentally, this example shows that far from its being the case that commitment excludes reflection and argument, as Bartley supposes, it is sometimes the case that only by reflection and argument does a man become aware of what he is committed to. People are not born empiricists or utilitarians or Barthians. If they take up such positions they may do so after thought. Something like a rational process goes on. It is necessary to distinguish such cases from others where we might say that no rational process has gone on. To take an example: there is a difference between a man who becomes committed religiously as a result of being subjected to emotional evangelical preaching, or politically as a result of brain-washing, and a scholar who after years of studying theology or philosophy decides that he is a Barthian or an empiricist. Bartley writes: 'The fundamental problem of modern philosophy . . . is the problem of . . . showing that it is possible to choose in a nonarbitrary way among competing, mutually exclusive theories, and—more broadly speaking—among competing "ways of life"' (Bartley, p. 105). It is clear that he sees commitment as always arbitrary. It is surely the case, however, that we can and do distinguish between arbitrary commitment and non-arbitrary commitment. Given that a man is, say, an empiricist, he may well be described as committed to the empiricist principle, but the process of getting there need not be described only by terms like 'arbitrary', 'irrational', etc. Furthermore, once there, a man may defend his commitment by argument in at least the negative sense that he may try to point to logical inconsistencies in other positions. Admittedly such argument does not prove his own position, but it is meant to have the effect of strengthening his position as against the others. At any rate it is a *rational* procedure, within Bartley's own terms. Of people who prefer to remain 'irrationalists' Bartley writes: 'It may be difficult indeed to argue with any such person, for he will have abandoned argument' (Bartley, p. 216). This is extreme. It comes from lumping together as irrationalists everyone who is committed to some ultimate principle. But we can distinguish among such people.

Commitment does not necessarily mean the abandonment of logic or argument.

There is in religion a kind of commitment, that does not exclude criticism, but that sometimes has to be accepted as over-riding criticism. This is a large part of what is meant by *faith*. (Compare what Professor Basil Mitchell says in his parable of the stranger—see Flew and MacIntyre, pp. 103–5.) The case is somewhat similar with morality. We do not hold our moral principles as hypotheses, to be tested by experience. ('Let us consider the hypothesis that Hitler was right to try to exterminate the Jews.') Moral principles are principles that we are committed to. There could be a religion of hypotheses, a religion of conjecture and refutation; but it would not be Christianity. Christianity involves commitment of several sorts—to a person, to a course of action, to a whole way of life, to a set of propositional beliefs.

On the other hand, that religion involves commitment does not conflict with the possibility of religious doubt, any more than the kind of commitment involved in knowledge is incompatible with oscillations of uncertainty.

The Popper–Bartley view has the effect of ruling out the possibility of combining commitment and rationality. Bartley's view, as I have indicated, seems to me a mistaken one. In the present book the position adopted is one in which the commitment which, it must be acknowledged, is a part of religious belief is presented as not incompatible with rationality.

If the position which Bartley has developed were correct, then (given a certain assumption about religion) it could be developed into a *demonstration* of something often maintained, namely, that religion is fundamentally non-rational. In many writers, religion is presented as in part rational, in part non-rational. According to Bartley's position, however, it would seem to be necessary to choose between the following alternatives: either religion is fundamentally irrational, because based on commitment; or, if it is to be in any degree rational, it must be seen as not based upon commitment but as a set of correctible hypotheses. My criticism of Bartley has been intended to suggest that the choice he offers is an over-simplified one. A basis for religion in commitment is not incompatible with religion's being rational, or, indeed, with the basis in commitment being rationally arrived at or rationally defensible. What is also important is the rejection of the alternative that religion, to be respectable, must take the form exclusively of a set of correctible hypotheses. I should claim that this must be rejected if the philosophy of religion is to be recognisably the philosophy of the Christian religion: at any rate, it puts the matter over-simply (see Chapter 7, section 2).

2

BELIEF AND SCEPTICISM

1. *Deciding to believe*

What we believe is balanced by what we doubt; reasons for doubting take their place together with reasons for believing. Belief is complemented by doubt in the thinking of religious believers themselves. Accounts of the lives of religious people sometimes refer to periods during which they had to struggle to maintain belief in the face of pressing doubts.

It is usually maintained that (to adopt a convenient formulation) 'belief is not an affair of the will'. Locke, for instance, in urging religious toleration upon civil magistrates, remarks that in any case it is impossible to enforce articles of faith by law. 'For it is absurd that things should be enjoined by laws which are not in men's power to perform. And to believe this or that to be true, does not depend upon our will' (Locke, p. 150). A similar point is made by Professor H. D. Lewis in the course of a discussion of religious commitment. 'We do not strictly choose to believe at all—in any sphere. . . . I do not choose to believe that the grass is green. I can believe nothing else, the evidence of my eyes and all other evidence being what it is. I should be mad if I said that I chose after all that it should be red, and even my form of speech would be incorrect. I do not choose that twice two is four, I can do no other than believe that it is' (Lewis, pp. 54–5). And Stuart Hampshire writes:

In the case of belief, it is not clear what counts as trying and intending to believe something, but failing in the attempt, although these phrases are sometimes used. I may well say in ordinary conversation 'I want to believe what you are telling me, but I cannot'. But the statement of a difficulty in the 'attempt' is already a statement that I do not believe and is not seriously meant. . . . 'I have finally made myself believe him', or 'I am

determined to believe whatever he tells me', are virtually professions of
scepticism. . . . [W]hen a statement is brought to my attention, and the
question is whether I believe it or not, the decision that I announce in
the words 'Yes, I believe it' is not a decision to do anything; nor can these
words constitute an announcement that I have attempted or achieved
anything. I have not decided *to* believe; I have decided *that* the statement
in question is true (Hampshire, pp. 157–8).

Undoubtedly there is the religious phenomenon commonly
described as that of struggling to overcome doubts and to maintain
religious belief. It might be said that the accounts of this (alleged)
phenomenon are mis-descriptions: that what is happening in a man
in such a case is, for example, a struggle to prevent himself from
dwelling upon certain sceptical thoughts, but not a struggle to prevent
himself from ceasing to believe something. The notions of making
oneself believe something, or preventing oneself from ceasing to believe
something, are undeniably odd. We recognise that the White Queen
is meant to sound absurd when she claims to have been able by
practice to believe six impossible things before breakfast; we resist
the suggestion that she could *set herself* to believe something,
impossible or otherwise. Certainly, if we take Lewis's example,
'I do not choose to believe that the grass is green', we may readily
agree that this is so; the greenness of grass is not the sort of thing
that we *choose* to believe or not believe. But whatever is to be said
about belief, religious *commitment* is something that it does not seem
improper to describe as sometimes 'an affair of the will'. Rational
commitment—commitment that follows a possibly lengthy process
of weighing-up various considerations—might sometimes be said
to be 'an affair of the will'. A man who commits himself in this way,
as opposed to one who 'merely' (without much thought) commits
himself, could be said to be *deciding upon* or *choosing* a commitment,
or *deciding* or *choosing* to devote himself to a certain cause. Both
in maintaining faith in the face of returning doubts and also in the
original commitment to religious belief it would seem to be possible
to say, if one wishes to use this terminology, that the will is active.
There are religious believers who never suffer from doubts, as there
are believers who just grow into religious commitment. If all religious
believers were like this then religious commitment might with more
plausibility be said never to be an affair of the will. But they are not
all like this.

It might be objected that it is not the becoming committed to
something that can be 'an affair of the will' so much as the preliminary process of thinking about the matter. That is to say, what we
may *decide* to do is to reflect upon various considerations, perhaps
if we are rather calculating to weigh up the advantages to ourselves

of commitment to Communism or to Catholicism, etc., but we do not *decide to commit* ourselves: it is rather that we may *find ourselves*, at the end of the process of thought, committed to something. We do not decide upon or choose a commitment; all we can decide upon or choose is, before we are committed, to examine the pros and cons as carefully as we are able. I should reply, however, that we do (as Hampshire himself acknowledges in the case of belief) frequently and naturally speak of commitment itself in terms of something that a man in some sense *does* (formally: 'I hereby commit myself . . .') as opposed to a condition in which he finds himself—perhaps most naturally in cases where there seem to be alternatives. The notions of belief and commitment are not identical; and although I do not take issue with the view that we do not choose to believe, I should not read this as meaning that we cannot choose to commit ourselves. And as far as religion is concerned, the notion of commitment is a central one. (On belief and the will see also the discussion of the 'infused' virtue of faith, in Chapter 5, section 4.)

2. *Religious doubt and religious scepticism*

An examination of religious belief needs to concern itself with religious doubt and scepticism. A study of non-belief (in particular, of 'active' non-belief as opposed to mere indifference to religion) we may reasonably expect to throw light upon religious belief. We may be reminded of Mill's defence (in *On Liberty*) of the view that unless the holder of any set of beliefs suffers the free circulation of contrary opinions he will be in danger of not understanding fully what he himself claims to believe, and in danger also of not being able to justify his beliefs, supposing he wants to justify them. Although, in general, a man is not bound to justify his beliefs, he will in practice be likely to want to justify those of them that he considers to be important and to have a bearing upon life, and also those that he may want other people to share. Religious beliefs are of this kind. It is by defending his position against others that a man best becomes clear about his own views and their ground; it may even be that it is only in this way that such clarity can really be achieved. But, as we have already noted, the believer and the doubter are not always externally opposed to one another. Sometimes the believer is his own doubter. He may want to maintain his belief in opposition to his own doubts, not those of others.

A distinction may be drawn between religious scepticism and religious doubt. The former seems to bear the stronger sense. There is an implication here of possible hostility, or at any rate of lack of sympathy. Perhaps the sceptic is a hard man to convince because he does not want to be convinced. The religious believer may be allowed to entertain religious doubts; but for a man to be seriously described as both a believer and a sceptic would suggest a split personality. The difficulties that the believer has in maintaining his belief will often be different from those which ensure the sceptic's remaining a sceptic. The believer's doubt even whether God exists, for example, though it might on some occasions be not greatly different from the sceptic's scepticism about the existence of God, will sometimes be very different indeed, as the longing of a mother for her dead child is different from the desire of a childless woman to have a child. The religious believer is involved, as the sceptic is not. To be committed and yet to have doubts is not the same as not to be committed at all. The sceptic is typically an outsider, the doubter an insider. It might be said that the sceptic, because typically his emotions are not involved and because he is not already committed to the beliefs he is questioning, is more likely than the religious believer to give difficulties their due weight. It is certainly the case that religious apologetic writing sometimes contains quantities of what looks like special pleading. On the other hand, the sceptic, as an outsider, may miss things that are of religious significance. He may be seeing clearly but (from the point of view of the believer) he may be seeing superficially. He may assimilate what the religious believer says to categories that he, the sceptic, already possesses, but which, naturally, include none peculiar to religious discourse. (As Kierkegaard said, what the knight of faith sees as sacrifice the merely moral man can only see as murder.) We have already noted the way in which Ayer assigned the mystic to the category of people who intend to convey information, and found him wanting because he does not succeed in doing this very well. Of course, the sceptic can cut his way through a great deal of dead wood, but he may in doing so ignore differences between trees that for some other purposes may be of considerable importance: it can even be that a tree which is dead from his point of view is, from that of someone else, alive.

It might be said that the contrast I am drawing between the sceptic and the believer-with-doubts is too unsubtle, and that I am assuming someone who *adopts the attitude of* a sceptic, and approaches religion from the outset with a determination to find fault. Surely, it might be said, not all the people called sceptics advance upon religion in an unsympathetically critical spirit. Are there not some whose scepticism is consequent upon their consideration of difficulties, rather than something which conditions their approach to religion?

It is hard to maintain a neutral position. ('He that is not with me is against me' presumably applies to philosophers of religion as well as other men.) Writers on the philosophy of religion may see themselves as aiming to demolish or defend, and not merely to analyse and clarify, religious belief. If the issues involved are worth examining seriously they are presumably worth taking sides on. Anyone who is likely to be attracted to this field is likely also to be inclined towards one attitude to it rather than another. And we are not bound to suppose that the differences between philosophers of religion have nothing whatever to do with their antecedent attitudes within or towards religion. Indeed, it is not easy to see why complete neutrality in this field should be thought to be a virtue—if it is. At the same time, it is hardly necessary to say that there is more than one middle way between neutrality and commitment—between, on the one hand, total non-involvement, a refusal to take sides, a limitation of interest to the defining of concepts and the careful weighing-up of arguments, etc., and, on the other hand, a determined promulgation of a committed position, a refusal to see the other side, even a twisting of facts to suit one's purposes, etc.

The sceptic and the reflective self-critical religious believer use the same logical tools when they examine religious arguments and concepts, yet either may assert a significance that the other denies. The differences between them are not to be settled by logic alone, and in the end some of them are not to be settled at all.

3. *Agnosticism*

Alongside scepticism and religious doubt we need to take account of agnosticism. Agnosticism need not be merely a matter of professed ignorance about whether or not God exists. For someone to claim to be an agnostic can sometimes argue a fair degree of interest in religion; and whereas in politics the 'don't knows' may also be the 'don't cares', in religion agnosticism can be itself a particular view or school of thought. The agnostic's claim not to know can be not merely negative but part of a set of positive beliefs about the impossibility of attaining knowledge of God. Agnosticism can even be a 'way of life'. Agnosticism, in short, seems to carry more of the suggestion of a set of doctrines about religion and a definite attitude towards it than do scepticism or religious doubt, which might easily be piecemeal in character

Religious agnosticism is the view held within religion that God is 'beyond our comprehension'. The point of calling it 'religious' agnosticism is to imply a contrast with 'anti-religious' agnosticism. The view I have in mind in using the expression 'religious agnosticism' is not that of people who are disposed to reject religious belief but do not consider themselves justified in unequivocally denying the existence of God; it is rather the view of those who are disposed to

believe in God but who tend to express their belief as being in 'the
Great Unknown', 'the Unconditioned', or the like (compare Matthew
Arnold's 'the eternal not ourselves which makes for righteousness').
The notion of God as being beyond the limits of human knowledge—
developed from Kant by Cousin and by Hamilton ('the philosophy
of the unconditioned') and by Mansel in his 1858 Bampton Lectures
on 'the limits of religious thought'—was a familiar one in the nineteenth century, and has reappeared in somewhat different form in
the twentieth in Otto's *The Idea of the Holy*.

The view that God is 'unknowable' needs to be argued for: it
might be claimed that if God is infinite then it follows immediately
that he must be beyond human understanding, for 'infinite', *contra*
Descartes, does not name a positive property possessed by God but
means 'beyond our powers of comprehension or description'. But
whatever arguments might be offered, they are open to examination.
Supposing it to be argued for the sake of argument that God is
unknowable, it is then necessary to consider various items of religious
belief on their merits. Not all religious belief concerns the existence
or nature of God. Some of it is purely factual belief about the life
and teachings of Jesus; and some is belief in moral principles. It
would not follow from the unknowability of God that beliefs of
either of these two types ought or ought not to be accepted. It is
possible to hold a religious view, though it would not be orthodox
Christianity, which is agnostic about God and which consists partly
in entertaining certain beliefs about the life and teachings of Jesus
and partly in an adherence to Christian moral principles; such a
view (that of Professor R. B. Braithwaite) will be considered in the
following chapter.

I have been writing indifferently of the view that God is 'unknowable' and the view that God is 'beyond our comprehension', but in the
remainder of the discussion in this section I shall concentrate mainly
on the latter: the matter to be considered here is chiefly what is
involved in saying that we do not or cannot understand or compre-
hend God rather than what is involved in saying that we do not or
cannot know that God exists. The status of the 'metaphysical' part
of religious belief, including beliefs about the existence and nature
of God and the relation of God to the world, has been disputed.
Reductionist views, of which Braithwaite's is one, commonly
aim to give an account of religion in which this metaphysical part
does not figure at all or is transformed into something else. 'Reductionist' is perhaps a pejorative word. I do not intend, however, in
using it to suggest either that I am myself taking up any particular
attitude towards any view so labelled or that there might not be
more favourable ways of referring to such views; nor am I prejudging

the question whether any such view is correct or incorrect—each would need to be examined on its merits.) Bultmann's 'de-mythologi-sing' of religion, Bonhoeffer's 'religionless Christianity', the 'Death of God' school of theology—these are all attempts to interpret religion without its 'metaphysical' element. Religious agnosticism takes its place in a corner of the same general picture. It has a strong historical basis, for it goes back in fact far beyond Kant, having some of its roots in the *via negativa*, and it received an expression in the seventeenth century from Hobbes.

But religious agnosticism is only one strand in the Christian tradition. Christian theology and religion have traditionally had much to say about the nature of God, and it would hardly do to set all this on one side on the general ground that the notion of God is beyond our comprehension. The traditional position would seem to be that God is not *wholly* beyond human comprehension. Much can be said about God, and both the theologian and the philosopher of religion are involved in the study of how it is possible to say of God the things that it is agreed can be said (can be said, because they *are* said). Nevertheless, agnosticism is a sufficiently important strand in Christian religion and theology to merit further discussion here.

One thing that might be meant by the claim that God is beyond human comprehension is that God cannot be spoken about except by myth, analogy, etc. A fairly strong version of this is the view that God can only be spoken about in paradoxes. Paradoxes may con-cern situations in 'the real world', but the situations themselves are not paradoxical; the paradox typically comes into being through the use of a particular form of words in the statement of the situa-tion, and may be resolved through a decision to state it in some other form of words (cf. the paradox of the liar). Paradox in poetry is similarly *created*, and can be similarly removed—though, of course, if another form of words is adopted the *poetry* may well be destroyed. The point to note is that the paradox lies not in situations themselves but in the language that men choose to use to describe those situa-tions; even though in the case of poetry the writer may be quite likely to say that his paradoxes are forced upon him, in the sense that he can find no non-paradoxical form of words that seems adequate to what he wants to say, which would not be the case with the deviser of a logical paradox like the paradox of the liar. The paradoxes of religion might be like those of the poet. But this would give no real support to religious agnosticism. Perhaps only paradoxical language would be adequate for talk about God; but, clearly, to hold that we seem unable to say what we want to say about God in non-paradoxical language does not mean that *God* is incomprehensible. Presumably for this we should need to be able

to say that the paradoxical language reflects a parado
affairs'. But the notion of things or situations (or God
doxical seems to be a metaphorical one: we cannot sup
existence of paradoxical forms of words that they are li
tions of paradoxical situations (whatever those might
paradoxical descriptions of (mere) situations.

It does not follow from the fact alone, if it is a fact, t
tional theistic arguments or 'proofs' are invalid, that God's existence
could never be proved, though that might seem a plausible supposition; but although the failure of the theistic arguments does not
provide grounds for atheism, as would a valid argument, if such
there were, to the non-existence of God, it might well be seen as
providing grounds for agnosticism by anyone who was disposed to
put much weight on proof of God's existence. Again, however,
it is hard to see that this offers any strong foundation for agnosticism.
God might be beyond argument but not beyond experience. Theistic
proofs are not necessary for belief in God or comprehension of God;
and those who have claimed belief in God have probably seldom
supposed their belief to rest upon theistic arguments. And there seems
no good reason to suppose that if God's existence is 'beyond argument' God is therefore not comprehensible.

The position developed by Hamilton and Mansel depends upon
the view that to know is to 'condition'. God, being unconditioned,
is consequently unknowable; what, if anything, would be known
by someone who claimed knowledge of God could not be *God*.
Some analogies come to mind. As a person grows older and his
experience of life and the world expands there are fewer things that
it is possible for him to experience for the first time, fewer things
to *discover*. Once discovered, *Middlemarch*, or *Das Lied von der
Erde*, are impossible to discover again. Similarly, once one has solved
a puzzle it is no longer a puzzle: unless we totally forget its solution
it is impossible ever to *solve* it again; possible only to go through the
motions of 'solving' it. Once the great novel or the great piece of
music, or even the crossword puzzle, has been absorbed by us, it
can never be regarded in quite the same way again. It might be
held that God is only God while unknown. And one might then go
on to say that to attempt to *explain* and to *understand* God would be
to break down the distance and strangeness from us that is part of
our notion of God. One motive for religious agnosticism might
then be the belief that only an unknown God is adequately *God*.
Perhaps only the man who refuses to claim understanding of God
has a proper conception of God; for what must be said of God, if
God is to be an adequate object of worship, might be that God is
beyond our understanding. (Compare the view of Professor J. N.

c

ndlay that only a non-existent God would be worth worshipping—see Flew and MacIntyre, p. 74. Where Findlay is suggesting that only the atheist has an adequate religious attitude, the foregoing passage suggests that only the agnostic has.)

There are degrees of agnosticism. At one extreme there is the person who claims that while he has no certain *knowledge* in this field he does have *beliefs* to which he clings as a matter of faith. Agnosticism in this sense is a characteristic of practically all religious people; and the beliefs that such an agnostic holds might be quite numerous. At the other extreme there is the person who claims that he himself can see no ground for holding any religious *beliefs* whatever. (We are concerned here not with persons who have no interest in religion, but rather with those who have such an interest and have arrived at the latter extreme agnostic position as a result of reflection.) In between come the majority of those who would be likely to be given, or to give themselves, the label 'agnostic'.

Religious agnosticism bears some of the marks of wanting to have the best of two worlds. I am not thinking now of the person who adopts what may be called a religious attitude to the world but who does not consider himself entitled to adhere to theism, but rather of the person who adopts a vague kind of theism, centring upon notions like those mentioned earlier—'the Wholly Other', 'the Unknown', and we may add 'the Transcendent'. As long as no claim is made to knowledge of, or even belief in, God, most of the problems about the understanding of the notion of God naturally in practice do not arise. But if expressions like 'the Wholly Other', 'the Transcendent', are to be intelligible, some account needs to be given of their meaning. Are they the *names* of something? If so, of what? The difficulties which have led to the adoption of an agnostic position about God are not solved by substituting other terms for 'God'. These seem to be merely synonyms for 'God', or for some part of the meaning of 'God', and the old difficulties therefore largely remain. That they are no more than synonyms for 'God' is suggested by the impossibility of taking literally terms like 'the Unknown' or 'the Wholly Other'. If indeed nothing is known of 'the Unknown', or if 'the Wholly Other' is indeed wholly other, the user of such expressions cannot easily assume that they refer to any identifiable entity. In order for us to have the relation of being-ignorant-of to some entity it must be possible to identify that entity: knowing nothing of, or being ignorant of, is a matter of knowing nothing of (the existence of) X, where X is independently specifiable, or being ignorant of the truth of p where p is specifiable. 'The Unknown' or 'the Wholly Other' cannot literally be entirely unknown or entirely other. It would be absurd to pretend to refer to a thing or a notion which at the same time you want to say cannot be identified in any way. Some characterisation of the Unknown or the Wholly Other follows (explicitly or implicitly) and given that such terms are used by religious writers in religious contexts it would not be surprising if what is said about the Unknown or the Wholly Other—for example, about the Wholly Other or 'the Transcendent' as an object (or objects: for are these the same or different?) of worship—bears a close resemblance to what is said by an orthodox Christian theist about God.

Religious agnosticism is unlikely to be—and indeed never could be—complete. It is sometimes a strand within religious belief, helping to make up the whole, and sometimes a kind of independent religious position: in neither case, however, does the religious agnostic consider himself precluded from saying things about God or about other religious matters. It is therefore not necessary to decide whether agnosticism is a *correct* view about religion before proceeding further with the discussion of religious belief. Even supposing one were convinced that religious agnosticism is the proper view to take about religion, the task of examining religious beliefs would still to some extent remain, for religious agnostics will still in practice offer some characterisation of that which they deny understanding of. Although we may claim no understanding of X we must be able to identify what it is that we are claiming to have no understanding of—and it is a short distance then to giving some account of X, however minimal.

4. *Religion and verificationism*

Either the sceptic considers he has reason for suspecting the intelligibility of what religious believers say, or he considers he has reason for doubting its truth. That is, he may maintain that religious belief cannot be understood, that it is (or, more strictly, that some parts of it are) meaningless or self-contradictory; or he may maintain that although he can understand it, it is (or again, some parts of it are) false.

For example, in the matter of intelligibility, the doctrine of the Trinity has been held to be an impossible one (see Durrant [2]). Again, the notion of necessary existence or of a necessary being has been criticised, both on the ground that existence, however qualified, is not an attribute of anything (if this means a property possessed by it) and on the ground that in any case necessity is a notion meaningful only in relation to propositions (i.e. logical necessity) not things. The intelligibility of the notion of God has been doubted also on the ground of apparent mutual incompatibility between such alleged divine attributes as justice and mercy, love and impassibility. (We shall take up these matters again in Chapter 4, section 1.) But supposing that religious beliefs are intelligible, are not many of them simply false?

We have already had occasion to note that there are various kinds of Christian religious beliefs: factual, moral, and metaphysical. As far as purely factual beliefs are concerned (e.g. the belief that Jesus was born in Bethlehem, or even that he existed at all; or the belief that he taught such-and-such things) the issue of truth or falsehood is a fairly straightforward one. Either Jesus was born in Bethlehem or he was born elsewhere; either he existed as a person, as Christians believe, or he did not exist (but is perhaps only the personification of a mushroom, as has been alleged). If he existed, either he did in fact utter the Aramaic equivalent of 'Thou shalt love thy neighbour as thyself' or he is misreported as having done so. If doubts are cast on factual religious beliefs there is at least no doubt as to what is meant by the assertion that such beliefs are false, and there is no doubt as to the way in which, at any rate in principle, one could go about establishing their truth or falsehood. Of course, in practice, as opposed to principle, it may well be extremely difficult, if not impossible, to establish finally the truth or falsehood of a given factual religious belief: everything may depend upon certain records whose trustworthiness is in doubt and likely to continue to be. Speculation about the psychology of, and social influences upon, people of a culture long dead and very different from our own may also be called for. But although the actual establishing of the truth or falsehood of a given historical statement may not be a simple matter, nevertheless the historical statements that I have in mind concern events or situations of a straightforward kind, as opposed, say, to statements which involve such uncertainties as a ruler's possible motive in making a certain alliance; and whatever difficulties there may be in getting agreement on whether such events or situations are accurately reported in the religious beliefs that purport to report them, at any rate there is no great difficulty in the notion of their being true or false.

When we come to the moral element in religious belief the situation is different. Although it is a matter of fact whether Jesus did or did not teach such-and-such moral principles, the moral principles themselves are neither matters of fact nor statements of fact. However, we need not for our present purposes consider the moral element in religion. It is not generally about this that sceptics are sceptical. And sceptics are, indeed, seldom much concerned to be sceptical about the factual element in religious belief—or, at any rate, philosophical sceptics are not. The reasons for this are obvious enough. In order to be sceptical about alleged matters of historical fact a considerable expertise is necessary, an expertise that is unlikely to be part of the equipment of many philosophers. Scepticism of this kind is in any case no part of the philosopher's business. The philosopher's concern is chiefly with arguments and with concepts. Questions of fact can generally be left to the experts in particular fields. The philosopher has his own field of expert knowledge of a kind at least partly factual, namely the history of philosophy itself, but in the field of the origins of Christianity he can claim no particular knowledge as philosopher.

We are left with the metaphysical element in religious belief as the field where the sceptic can, and does, mainly exercise his scepticism. The metaphysical element consists of what appear to be assertions about the existence of God, the attributes of God, God's relation to Jesus, God's relation to the universe and particularly to man, etc. It has sometimes been claimed by religious believers that such assertions are supportable by evidence. Thus the existence of God, it has been claimed, is provable by consideration of evidence of design in the universe. (On the Argument from Design see Chapter 4, section 3.) That God is concerned in a benevolent way with the affairs of men, it is claimed, can be shown from the evidence of miracles. (On miracle, see Chapter 5, section 1.) Hume, a good example of someone who has commonly been labelled 'sceptic', in his two most famous discussions of religion deals with just these two matters.

Professor Antony Flew has maintained (in effect) that 'sophisticated religious people' are inconsistent in their reliance upon evidence: they accept evidence that seems to support their case and reject that which does not (see Flew and MacIntyre, pp. 96–9). Flew's argument is as follows. Religious believers utter sentences like 'God has a plan', 'God created the world', 'God loves us as a father loves his children'. But when evidence is brought forward that seems to tell against such utterances—for example, a child suffering from inoperable cancer—far from abandoning their belief the religious believers qualify it in some such way as 'God's love is not a merely human love'. What appears to be at the outset a straightforward assertion ('God loves us'), under pressure of the piling up of apparent evidence to the contrary, is progressively qualified until in the end it seems that whatever happens the believer will go on saying 'God loves us (but with qualifications)'. But if no state of affairs is to be allowed to count decisively against the 'assertion' that God loves us then this 'assertion' is not an assertion at all; for when we assert that something is the case we mean to exclude certain possibilities—in particular, that what would be asserted by the denial of the original assertion is *not* the case. An assertion that does not imply the denial of anything is not an assertion at all. Flew puts the challenge: 'What would have to occur or to have occurred to constitute for you a disproof of the love of, or of the existence of, God?' (Flew and MacIntyre, p. 99). Unless this challenge can be met the implication is that the utterance 'God loves us' must be seen as not a genuine assertion at all. (Taken as a whole, Flew's argument is concerned with the meaningfulness of religious beliefs more than with their truth, but it does also bear upon the latter.)

If evidence is relevant at all, then all evidence must be taken into account, whether it is for or against. We may take three ways of looking at religious propositional beliefs: (1) evidence is relevant and must be allowed to count both in their favour and against; (2) the only evidence allowable as relevant is evidence that tends to show them to be true, and whatever may seem to tend to show them as false is not evidence (this is the position that Flew rejects, though it is doubtful whether he is correct in supposing that it is the position taken up by what he calls 'sophisticated' religious believers [Flew and MacIntyre, p. 98], as opposed to one taken up by some religious believers); (3) they are to be adopted or rejected on grounds other than the adducing of 'evidence'. Of these three positions the second is clearly unallowable, for it makes a mockery of evidence. But either of the other two positions is possible. I discuss the issues here more fully in the final chapter. On the face of it, the third would seem to fit the Christian tradition better than the first. Some analyses of religious belief attempt to meet the implications of the position that religious utterances are not genuine assertions by presenting them under various non-assertoric umbrellas: they are committings of oneself in faith, or indications of attitude, or they are in reality moral utterances. The last of these, in one version, will be examined at length in the next chapter. Such views are implausible to the extent that religious beliefs look like assertions. How can it have come about that men have so deceived themselves for centuries? How can they have fallen into the habit of expressing as grammatical assertions what are logically quite different kinds of utterance? A simpler view would consist in resisting the suggestion that religious beliefs cannot be assertions because (some) religious believers will not admit anything as tending to count against them: what follows from the behaviour of such believers is not necessarily only that what they say cannot be counted as genuine assertions; it can equally well be said that such believers are inconsistent. It would seem to be a matter of fact that not all believers are like these. (I have discussed the views of Flew himself elsewhere—see McPherson [1], chapter 12. And see the discussion by Heimbeck, especially chapter III.)

5. Conflicts of religious truth-claims

Scepticism about religious beliefs might seem to draw support from the existence of many widely different religious traditions.

Problems of understanding religious beliefs are likely to be somewhat different depending on whether one is considering them from 'inside' or from 'outside'. On the one hand, there is the point of view of someone who himself belongs within a given tradition—here the Christian tradition—and who has difficulties about the understanding, and perhaps the reconciling, of beliefs within that tradition. In putting the matter in this way I do not intend at the present stage of the discussion to refer only to those who accept the beliefs in question. Critics of such beliefs (in the present case, atheists, non-religious agnostics, and others) also belong within what is broadly the same tradition. Their criticism can be regarded as criticism from within, much as is that of the theologian writing critically about the views of a fellow-theologian. On the other hand, there is the point of view of someone outside a given tradition, someone in the position of the social anthropologist, who attempts to understand the religious beliefs of that tradition. From this latter point of view, disputes over matters of religious belief between Christian believers and atheists or sceptics, as much as such disputes among Christian believers themselves, may appear as domestic disputes, something to be noted but not something that the observer would think it proper himself to pass judgement on. The distinction as I have drawn it is no doubt sharper than one finds it in fact: the sceptic sometimes approaches religious belief as if believers inhabited another planet, and the social anthropologist may sometimes want to condemn or approve what he observes. Nevertheless, there is, broadly, a distinction of the kind I have mentioned.

The question arises, how far it is proper to limit an examination of religious beliefs to a particular tradition, in this case the Christian tradition? What importance, if any, should be allowed to conflicts, if any exist, between Christian religious beliefs and the beliefs of other religions? The kind of conflict that might chiefly seem to call for some consideration is that between rival *truth-claims* of different religions. Supposing there to be a direct conflict between a truth-claim of religion A and a truth-claim of religion B, there might well be a logical obstacle to acceptance of one or the other: both truth-claims, presumably, could not be true. We need to consider how far there is a problem about reconciling the truth-claims of Christianity with those of other religions. It would certainly seem to be a reason for questioning religious beliefs if it were the case that religious men in other traditions maintained very different things.

We need to note that although we are concerned here with the possible existence of rival truth-claims we are concerned also with something else. Granted that there are rival truth-claims in some field it will not always be the case that this creates any problem. Generally speaking, there is a problem about the reconciliation of rival truth-claims when it is for some reason both difficult to reconcile them and important to have them reconciled. Some rivalries or apparent incompatibilities are more important than others. To ask whether there is a *problem* about reconciling them may well be to ask whether they are worth reconciling, whether anything valuable is to be achieved by reconciling them or anything valuable lost while they remain unreconciled. The Big Bang theory of creation is in conflict with the Steady State theory: this is a problem for cosmologists, and it is a problem because these are rival answers to what seems to them to be an important question. When one is asked whether there is a 'problem' about how certain rival truth-claims can be reconciled, one fairly natural reaction is to put two further questions: Does the conflict concern something important? and From whose point of view?

Conflicts between religions are not 'merely academic' issues. The issues here are important because they affect people's whole ways of life—the truth-claims of religion are bound up with claims about morality, etc., as we noted in the opening section of the first chapter. 'God is our Father' is a truth-claim of Christianity, and this claim is clearly linked with a certain policy, that of treating all men as brothers, and probably neither can be fully explicated apart from the other. Simply to ask whether 'God is our Father' is true or false is to have missed much of the point. If faced with the alternatives 'The teachings of Jesus are about how men should live' and 'The teachings of Jesus are about what men should believe, in isolation from how they should live', the Christian believer is likely to choose the former. To take into account the 'way of life' aspect of religion is not to take into account something *in addition to* its truth-claims. As I pointed out in the first chapter, it is necessary to consider the way of life aspect if the truth-claims themselves are to be understood. A study of the truth-claims of a religion that takes into account its moral and other principles is neither wandering from the point nor merely offering a kind of bonus. Nevertheless, in the interests of simplicity, let us try in what follows to isolate as far as may be possible the truth-claims from the wider way of life.

Those who think there is a problem about some particular rival truth-claims must understand, or believe they understand, the things that are being claimed in the rival truth-claims. There would seem to be several possibilities here. (1) The Christian who, let us say, holds claim p, may think that he understands claim q, which is made by some other religion, and may think that claim q is incompatible with claim p and that the incompatibility is important; whereas in fact claim q is not incompatible with claim p—i.e. he misunderstands claim q. In this case we have a problem without a real incompatibility. (2) The Christian may think he understands claim q and may think that claim q is compatible with claim p; whereas it is in fact incompatible with it. Then there is incompatibility without a problem. (3) The Christian may really understand claim q and may truly believe that it is incompatible with claim p and that the incompatibility is important. Then there is both an incompatibility and a problem. In other words, when faced with a question of the form, 'Is there a problem about the reconciliation of p and q?' where these are truth-claims, it is, sometimes at least, possible to separate the question whether there is a problem from the question whether there is an incompatibility. But this is complicated by the fact that in religion there are claims of a kind which many adherents of that religion would themselves say they do not fully understand or about whose meaning they may disagree. It is not always easy to establish whether truth-claims are in conflict because it is not always easy to be sure what is being claimed—that is, within Christianity, let alone as between Christianity and some other religion. In suggesting that one can separate the question whether there is a problem from the question whether there is an incompatibility, I do not wish to be taken as implying that one can always readily identify what is being claimed, and can set alongside each other in some straightforward way clearly-statable rival religious claims as if they were rival claims about matters of fact. The situation is hardly as simple as that.

A *problem* about reconciliation can arise if someone thinks he understands some truth-claims of another religion and thinks that they are importantly irreconcilable with some of those of his own. Nevertheless, suppose it to be the case that we cannot understand the claims of other religions, or can understand them only to a very small degree. If this were so, the reconciliation problem clearly ought to seem much less serious. If Christians were persuaded that only Hindus understand Hinduism, etc., then they would be likely to cease to think that there is a problem about the reconciliation of Christian and Hindu truth-claims. It seems reasonable, however, to assume that at least some degree of understanding of faiths other than one's own is possible. There are historical and conceptual continuities, at any rate between Christianity, Judaism and Islam. Further, all religions are religions. Someone who has begun to be a Christian comes to know something about religion and not just about Christianity. He acquires concepts, some of which he can bring to an understanding of some other religions—though not perhaps the same ones to all other religions. It is possible to admit this much without claiming—what would seem much less plausible—that all the religions of the world lie equally open to our understanding.

But let us consider more directly the question of how conflicts, if we suppose them to exist, can be solved. The very thing that gives rise to the conflict may also in a way provide a means for resolving it. While men were largely ignorant of religions other than their own, as long as they had no information, and not even misinformation, about other religions (if there ever was such a time), problems about the reconciliation of the claims of different religions naturally did not arise for them. But when such problems have once arisen, one way to settle them may lie in more information. The settling can take various forms: a synthesis of different claims (i.e. a search for 'the whole Truth'); or, perhaps, a recognition that there is so much diversity that one might as well live and let live religiously.

To suppose in connection with religion that by the clash of rival truth-claims more of 'the whole Truth' will emerge is to suppose that there is such a thing as 'the whole Truth' in religion. Is there? A chief difficulty is to know when we should have arrived at possession of 'the whole Truth' in religion. A subjective conviction of having attained the whole truth will hardly do; for we may have deceived ourselves. On the other hand, what tests could we apply? Is there an independently-held standard against which we could measure our progress towards the whole truth in religion? The standard will surely change and develop with the unfolding of more of the whole truth. To take a presumably analogous case: how do we know that we are developing *morally*? If we pass from a narrow legalistic morality to a freer kind of morality—a morality of love, let us say—we may recognise this as moral development in ourselves. But why do we say that the latter kind of morality is better, 'fuller', than the former? Presumably because, once we have moved on to the latter, our ideas of what a proper or 'developed' morality is have themselves been shaped by the influence of the latter morality upon us. The mystic may claim to have a deeper religious insight than the ordinary conventional believer. His notion of what religious insight is or ought to be is shaped by his mysticism, just as his mysticism is dependent to some extent on his initial grasping, through reading or example, of the possibility of such a thing as mystical experience. Exposure to other points of view within a religion, or exposure to other religions, like exposure to different and perhaps conflicting moral or political or aesthetic points of view, helps towards the cultivation of new standards and the recognition of new criteria of truth or excellence in these various fields. It would be extremely difficult to lay out a set of objective criteria, universally applicable, which we might apply in deciding which of two conflicting truth-claims in religion is true, or which of two ways of life is the more worth adhering to. But this is not to say that there are no criteria. The adherent of religion A, and the adherent of religion B, will each have his own ideas about what tests a religious truth-claim should be able to pass. To the extent that the adherent of religion A sympathetically studies religion B, so may his ideas about what is true or false in religion change, or, as he might himself say, develop. It is unfortunately the case that sometimes increased confrontations of different Christian denominations can lead to the reverse of understanding. But it seems safe to say that religious strife arises *more* from ignorance, and reconciliation *more* from deeper knowledge.

The view that I have been presenting is that there is a problem about how the truth-claims of Christianity can be reconciled with those of other religions to the extent that the Christian considers that there is an *important* conflict on some point. In a sense there might be said to be a reconciliation problem in every case of pairs of contrary or contradictory propositions. But the majority of such cases are not worth discussing. There is only a problem worth discussing—I have suggested, only a problem at all—when some *important* belief is at issue, when the denial of something can be shown to have important repercussions, etc. 'It is raining'—'No, it isn't'. It is hard to see how any problem is involved here. But: 'There is a God'—'No, there isn't', is another matter. If a Christian did not care very much whether men say 'There is a God' or 'There is no God', etc., then he would not have problems about the reconciliation of different religious truth-claims. However, an element of commitment undoubtedly enters into traditional Christianity, and it is hard to accept that a religion in which it did not matter very much what truth-claims a person made could properly be called Christianity. Whatever difficulties there may be about the identification or the interpretation of the claims of Christianity, it does make claims. Thus one way out of the problem is closed for the Christian believer. It would be implausible to say: there is no problem about how the truth-claims of Christianity can be reconciled with those of other religions, for Christianity makes no truth-claims. Individual Christians make very few; but Christianity makes some.

Another way out of the problem is by raising difficulties about understanding, either particular or general. If we come to see that we have misunderstood some particular claim made by another religion then the need for reconciliation may disappear. If we consider that we simply cannot understand another religion at all, again there will be no problem about reconciliation. As far as this kind of solution is concerned the objection is that we in fact do seem to be able to understand the claims of other religions, at any rate some of them and to some degree. There are difficulties, as we have seen, in the notion of a single religions Truth. At the same time, this notion could have some value if regarded as a kind of aspiration. 'There is a single religious Truth', or 'All religions point in the same direction' could function as encouraging slogans. Perhaps they are not to be taken as assertions, which must be either true or false, so much as expressions designed to encourage religious tolerance and sympathetic curiosity about other people's religious ways of life. (Though, as I said earlier about another case, it is a powerful objection to this that they *look* like assertions.) When faced with what might appear to be an incompatibility, the thought of such slogans would encourage the religious believer to try once again to see points of agreement as well as of difference. Of course, this would be to assume that it is a good thing for Christians to look for likenesses between Christianity and other religions.

It is perhaps worth remarking that the fact that religions may make different claims does not necessarily mean that they must be seen as making mutually incompatible claims: what they claim might simply not meet and hence not clash. In order to establish the existence of indubitably incompatible claims what would be needed is a close, detailed examination of specific claims made by different religions. The Muslim claim that no man is divine would seem to be incompatible with the Christian claim that Christ is both human and divine. Whether these actually are incompatible claims could only be settled by study of their meaning, each from the point of view of its own religion, and also each from the point of view of the other religion, and all of this requires a close acquaintance with other related claims (cf. Smart). As Christians dispute among themselves on the meaning of their claim, the discussion would probably be a lengthy one.

One point of relevance to the present discussion has not yet been mentioned. Many would take the Christian tradition to be maintaining that Christianity is about a unique revelation of God, unquestionably true, so that anything that contradicts it must be wrong. We may again draw an analogy with morality. A man's individual morality is something to which he is committed. Of course, morality is relative in the sense that people in different ages or in different places may hold somewhat different moral principles. But this does not mean that a man is not strongly committed to his own moral principles. Indeed, if he were not strongly committed to them they would not be his moral principles. Somewhat similarly, religion is relative in the sense that there are different religions and they do not all say the same thing. On the other hand, it does seem to be a mark of Christianity that the Christian is committed to certain beliefs. There is room for interpretation. There does not, however, seem to be room in the Christian tradition for a Christian's holding all the Christian claims purely as hypotheses.

3

SOME INTERPRETATIONS OF

RELIGIOUS BELIEF

1. *Religious language*

There is, as we have noted already, no single kind of religious utterance. At the same time, there are utterances which are of central importance in religion. The central utterances are those that I have earlier labelled 'metaphysical', and we have noted as examples 'God exists' and 'God loves us'. The term 'metaphysical' is being used here as a name for those religious utterances that are neither statements of empirical fact nor merely moral principles, and is not intended to close the door to closer examination.

Communication on religious matters between believer and believer is sometimes difficult, and communication between believer and non-believer much more so. As there are some people who cannot appreciate poetry—who cannot understand why the poet does not say what he wants to say in plain prose—so there are people who cannot, it seems, understand the language of religion. This is perhaps most obviously true in the case of those religious utterances which are prayers, or intended to indicate an attitude of reverence: some people do not understand the point of prayer, nor have they ever felt a need or desire to adopt an attitude of reverence towards anything. But it seems sometimes to be true also in the case of religious beliefs. A non-believer may simply not see the point of religious beliefs, like the man who does not see the point of poetry, or, to take a non-verbal case, like a man who has no appreciation of music beyond a few simple and obvious tunes. Such failure to understand is not necessarily permanent: after all, none of us is born appreciating poetry or seeing a point in religion. Understanding can be cultivated by good teaching, or come about through exposure to certain influences. Until understanding comes, communication between those within the religious circle and those without is undoubtedly not easy. Still, the fact that understanding can and often does come suggests that the language of religion is not *sui generis*. If it were, understanding would be more difficult than it is.

In any case, religious language uses ordinary words, whose everyday meaning is fixed by their use outside religion. 'Love' in 'God is love' presents in itself no difficulty in understanding, nor does 'father' in 'God is our Father'. Although religious language seems often to use ordinary words in extraordinary senses, it nevertheless does use ordinary words. There are enough links between the utterances of religious believers when they are expressing their religious beliefs and the utterances of anyone talking about everyday matters for it to be possible to say, though not without qualification, that the language of religion is not a special language. There are technical terms in theology, but neither religious nor theological language is marked by technical terms to anything like the extent of some other kinds of language. Perhaps if it were, matters would be simpler. It is because the religious believer expresses his beliefs to a large extent by using words whose associations are primarily with familiar human relationships and activities that some of the difficulties of understanding arise. There is, naturally, a temptation to want to take them at their face value. Yet this, it seems, will not do. God is our Father, yet not literally our father; God loves his children, yet not just as a human father loves his children; God created the world, but not as an artist creates a work of art. There is a tension between the desire to take utterances like 'God is our Father' literally and the conviction that, as God and not man is the subject of which fatherhood, etc., is predicated, they cannot be taken literally. The scholastic doctrine of analogy is an attempt to explain the use of ordinary everyday expressions in statements of religious belief. This is a technical doctrine and in any case does not meet the kind of scepticism about religious utterances that has been most influential in recent philosophical discussion (cf. Flew and Mac-Intyre, pp. 96–9). The doctrine of analogy does not meet the fundamental doubt whether religious beliefs are to be understood as assertions at all: it is rather concerned to show, on the assumption that they are assertions, *how* they assert. It is a doctrine that may be useful to believers who want to become clearer about the nature of their own belief; but it is not an answer to the sceptic who does not share its assumption that religious language is meaningful and needs only to have its meaning explicated: his doubt is more fundamental than that.

2. *A reductionist view of religious beliefs as moral beliefs*
We have so far in this book been more concerned with factual and

metaphysical religious utterances than with moral religious utterances. We have, indeed, assumed the factual and the metaphysical to be alternatives to each other: if the utterances expressing central religious beliefs are not to be classified as factual (or empirical) assertions but are still assertions then we have been supposing them to be metaphysical. But someone who comes to acknowledge, particularly if he does so with reluctance, that the most important religious utterances are not empirical is not necessarily going to take up without a struggle the position that they are metaphysical. To label them 'metaphysical' may seem to him tantamount to rejecting them as meaningless, such is the odium with which metaphysics has been regarded in some circles. If his attitude to religion is sympathetic, but he regards himself as an empiricist and is hostile towards metaphysics, it may strike him that the only viable alternative to the view of religious utterances as empirical is the view of them as moral. This is the position, already mentioned, of Professor Braithwaite, except that he would probably resist the word 'alternative', with its suggestion of a possible exclusive disjunction: religious beliefs he regards as a *mixture* of the empirical and the moral.

Braithwaite's view has often been called reductionist. The effect of his view is to reduce Christian religious belief to a combination of certain moral beliefs and certain empirical beliefs; though 'belief' he in fact regards as a somewhat inappropriate term, for he holds that the empirical 'beliefs' of religion need only to be entertained and not necessarily adhered to as true, and he holds further that the moral element is not properly a matter of moral beliefs but of practical intentions. Of the two elements the moral is the more important. It is here that Braithwaite finds the essence of religion. The empirical element comes in chiefly as a way of distinguishing between religions which seem to share the same or similar moral beliefs: the difference is found by noting that adherents of these religions will each entertain a different set of stories—the Christian a set of stories about Christ, the Muslim a set of stories about Mohamed, etc. The relatively minor part played by the empirical element (the 'stories') in Braithwaite's view is seen also in the fact that the connection between the adoption of a moral policy by a religious man and his entertaining of certain exemplary stories about Christ (or stories told by Christ—like the Parable of the Good Samaritan) is claimed by Braithwaite to be a causal or psychological, but not a logical, one. (An account of religious belief needs, I should maintain, to consider psychological as well as logical connections; but I think Braithwaite's own intention in suggesting that the connections referred to are causal or psychological rather than logical is to convey that *he* regards them as dispensable or, perhaps, as not possessing great philosophical importance.)

Braithwaite's starting point is a certain view of the nature of moral beliefs. (See Braithwaite; reprinted in Mitchell [3], to which page references are given.) This view is one which 'makes the primary use of a moral assertion that of expressing the intention of the asserter to act in a particular sort of way specified in the assertion' (Mitchell [3], p. 78). He then offers an 'assimilation of religious to moral assertions' (p. 80). 'The view which I put forward for your consideration is that the intention of a Christian to follow a Christian way of life is . . . the criterion for the meaningfulness of his assertions' (p. 80). It is important to note that the argument which he gives in favour of this view of moral beliefs is that it is the only view which answers satisfactorily the question: 'What is the reason for my doing what I think I ought to do?' He writes:

The answer it gives is that, since my thinking that I ought to do the action is my intention to do it if possible, the reason why I do the action is simply that I intend to do it, if possible. On every other ethical view there will be a mysterious gap to be filled somehow between the moral judgement and the intention to act in accordance with it: there is no such gap if the primary use of a moral assertion is to declare such an intention (p. 79). [He argues in a parallel way in defence of his view of religious assertions:] Unless a Christian's assertion that God is love (*agape*)—which I take to epitomize the assertions of the Christian religion—be taken to declare his intention to follow an agapeistic way of life, he could be asked what is the connection between the assertion and the intention, between Christian belief and Christian practice. And this question can always be asked if religious assertions are separated from conduct. Unless religious principles are moral principles, it makes no sense to speak of putting them into practice (p. 81).

The view is summed up as follows:

A moral belief is an intention to behave in a certain way: a religious belief is an intention to behave in a certain way (a moral belief) together with the entertainment of certain stories associated with the intention in the mind of the believer (p. 89). [Braithwaite goes on to say:] This solution of the problem of religious belief seems to me to do justice both to the empiricist's demand that meaning must be tied to empirical use and to the religious man's claim for his religious beliefs to be taken seriously (p. 89).

Now that Braithwaite's view has been outlined it is possible to proceed to discussion of it. Braithwaite is assimilating religious belief to a particular view of moral belief. This is not the place to go into discussion of rival views about moral belief, but it is relevant to remark that the view of moral belief that he presents would not be universally accepted. The virtue that he claims for it is that on

D

this view there is no gap between a moral judgement and the intention to act in accordance with it. It is true there would be no such gap, but the gap is got rid of by classifying moral judgements as 'primarily declarations of adherence to a policy of action, declarations of commitment to a way of life' (p. 80). Removing the fence between two fields is one way of ensuring that there is no longer a problem about how to get from one field to the other; but in becoming one, the two fields lose their separate identity. Where before they could each serve a different function, one pastoral the other arable, now one can take on the same use as the other and then in effect one of the formerly separate fields will have gained domination over the other. Although the view of moral judgements that sees them as 'primarily declarations of adherence to a policy of action' undoubtedly brings out an important function of some moral judgements, it is not acceptable as a view of moral judgements in general. Morality is not a matter only of action (duty, conduct): there is a whole vast class of moral judgements which are concerned with good rather than right, which pass judgements on states of affairs where action is not directly involved at all. (It is not possible to assume, without argument, that the judgement that such-and-such a state of affairs is good or bad entails that anyone should do anything about it. If there has been held to be a gap between moral judgements and intentions to act in accordance with them, there is also a gap between one class of moral judgements and another.) But even if we confine ourselves to moral judgements that are about action, it would still be implausible to suggest that all of these should be interpreted as declarations of intention. Many moral judgements are comments on other people's actions—by way of praising or blaming them—and need not be read as implying any intention on the part of the *speaker* to act in any particular way.

We might even say that Braithwaite has done a disservice to attempts to assimilate religious assertions to moral assertions by the particular way in which he goes about his own attempt. As we have seen, what he is attempting is in fact not simply the assimilation of religious to moral assertions but the assimilation of them to a particular theory about moral assertions. The objection to Braithwaite is not that religious assertions are not moral assertions, but that they are not moral assertions if *that* is what moral assertions are. We may now pursue this line of objection further by considering the four points of *difference* that Braithwaite acknowledges between religious and moral assertions; for Braithwaite, when he assimilates religious assertions to moral assertions, nevertheless does not wish to say that they are identical: it is possible to distinguish 'religious assertions from *purely* [my italics] moral ones' (p. 83). In the case of at least some of these differences what we have, I wish to maintain, are differences between religious assertions and moral assertions *on Braithwaite's view of moral assertions*. To acknowledge any differences at all is no doubt to weaken the basic position that religious assertions are to be assimilated to moral assertions. And if some of the differences are—as I shall hope to show—differences not so much between religious assertions and moral assertions as differences between religious assertions and moral assertions on a particular rather narrow view of the latter, then there would seem to be reason to doubt the adequacy of this particular assimilation of religious to moral assertions.

One difference mentioned by Braithwaite is that usually a whole set of religious assertions taken together specify the 'behaviour policy', whereas in morality commonly a single assertion does this. (At any rate, this is what I understand Braithwaite to be saying— see pp. 80–1, 82.) On Braithwaite's account of morality each (single) moral judgement presumably constitutes a declaration of intention. But there seems no reason why such a declaration of intention should not, in morality, be implied by a set of judgements, and equally no reason why in religion a man should not declare in a single statement his adherence to an agapeistic policy. (Braithwaite himself acknowledges that a single religious assertion may be 'representative of' or may 'epitomize' the whole system—p. 81.) There *is* a difference if morality is regarded as expressed primarily in individual commitments to action and religion as expressed primarily in a set or system of interrelated utterances. But there seems no good reason for thus regarding morality as less complex (or for that matter less social) than religion. There are always difficulties in assimilating something complex to something simple; but in this case the simplicity is an imposed one (on morality). A more plausible assimilation of religion to morality would seem to be achievable if both are allowed to be complex and likenesses pointed out here and there. There are moral principles and religious principles, moral rules and religious rules, moral judgements about states of affairs and religious judgements about states of affairs, moral judgements about particular actions and religious judgements about particular actions—and sometimes these are the same. There is individual and social morality, and individual and social religion— and in some respects these too are the same.

Another difference mentioned by Braithwaite is that in religion moral teaching is frequently given through concrete examples (like the Parable of the Good Samaritan) rather than in abstract terms. This seems, however, not to be a *difference*. Moral teaching by moralists who are not particularly aiming to expound religion is also given through concrete examples (stories like that of Gyges' ring in Plato's *Republic* lend themselves to this); and for that matter moral teaching within religion is also sometimes given in abstract terms (for example, the Beatitudes). Braithwaite in any case seems here to be mixing up two different levels. He contrasts in this respect the Parable of the Good Samaritan with Aristotle's doctrine of *eudaemonia* or Mill's of happiness. But this is to compare first-order Biblical religion, which is admittedly to a large extent concrete and not abstract (not 'philosophical') in expression, with what philosophers have said about morality, and philosophers usually write abstractly and not concretely. A fairer comparison would have been between theologians and philosophers (probably equally abstract) or between practical religious teachers and practical moral teachers (who might well be both equally 'concrete'). The moral philosopher tends to deal in general principles. The moral teacher may confine himself to stating particular cases. But the person who listens to both has the same task: that of translating what they say into terms applicable to himself.

The third difference mentioned by Braithwaite is that in religion

the conduct preached by the religion concerns not only external but also internal behaviour. The conversion involved in accepting a religion is a conversion, not only of the will, but of the heart. Christianity requires not only that you should behave towards your neighbour as if you loved him as yourself: it requires that you should love him as yourself (p. 83).

This only seems to be a difference between religion and morality if a certain view of morality is taken. As it happens, what is here said about religion is also frequently said about morality—that the truly moral man is not just someone who outwardly conforms to conventional moral standards but someone who is in a certain inward condition. Consider Kant's requirement that to have moral worth an action must be done out of a sense of duty. Kant was referring to actions, not to agents, but an analysis of this requirement needs to include reference to the inner attributes of agents. Again, an argument sometimes used against the legal enforcement of morality is that *morality* cannot be enforced, only outward conformity to moral standards; for 'morality itself' is something inward. (And compare what was said about belief and the will in the previous chapter. It is strange that Braithwaite himself should interpret morality in terms of intentions but at the same time imply that morality can be viewed as outward behaviour.) A full account of morality needs to make reference to this inward aspect as at least part of the whole account. It may appear that more stress is laid on the inward side by the Christian religion than by the morality of a Christian society; it is expected of a Christian that he love his neighbour, but it is enough in order for a man to be labelled a good man that he should behave as if he loves him. Yet outward behaviour is a sign of inward condition, and behaving well towards people is generally taken, in the absence of clear evidence to the contrary, to indicate an inner attitude of well-wishing.

The final difference between religious and (other) moral assertions is that 'a religious assertion will . . . have a propositional element which is lacking in a purely moral assertion, in that it will refer to a story as well as to an intention' (p. 84). It is here that we come to the empirical element in Braithwaite's account of religious belief. The religious believer need not, however, according to Braithwaite, as we have already noted, believe that the stories he associates with Christian moral principles are true. Further, as we have also noted, Braithwaite considers that the connection between these stories and the adoption of an agapeistic policy on the part of the Christian is causal or psychological, and not logical. Once again it can be remarked that as far as ordinary ground-level moral teaching is concerned there seems in fact to be no such difference between religion and morality. Many people associate the adopting of such-and-such a moral intention with thoughts about the behaviour and the words of admired individuals. If stories about Jesus do not run in the mind of a humanist (though they may) perhaps stories about Bertrand Russell do. In any case, this element in Braithwaite's theory is presumably not to be regarded as being of central importance. If religious beliefs are essentially intentions to adopt moral policies, and if Christian stories have only a causal or psychological connection with the adoption of Christian moral policies and not a logical one, it seems that it is not essential that the stories should be referred to in giving an account of the meaning of religious beliefs.

It may be remarked, however, that a very wide range of things is included by Braithwaite under the heading of Christian stories. They include interpretations of the doctrine of the Trinity (p. 88), also 'a pantheistic sub-set of stories in which everything is a part of God, and a dualistic Manichaean sub-set of stories well represented by St Ignatius Loyola's allegory of a conflict between the forces of righteousness under the banner of Christ and the forces of darkness under Lucifer's banner' (p. 88). They also include the 'story' that men in carrying out religious policies are doing the will of God. All these 'stories' are to be regarded as sets of propositions 'which are straightforwardly empirical propositions capable of empirical test' (p. 84). We are, that is, to limit ourselves to interpretations of the doctrine of the Trinity or of the Atonement that are empirical in character. But it is hard to see how it could be said of such interpretations that they are *adequate* interpretations. The Christian concept of God is not an empirical concept. Straightforwardly empirical stories cannot adequately represent God. I do not disagree with the view that to the extent that Christian moral beliefs may run parallel with those of, say, Buddhism, the place to look for differences between them is the other beliefs that are associated with them. Some of these other beliefs may well be 'straightforwardly empirical' ones. But others will be what I have referred to as metaphysical, which Braithwaite, on the basis of an empiricist dogma about meaning, admits only in the shape of empirical interpretations. If only moral beliefs and empirical beliefs are to be admitted as meaningful, then those religious beliefs that do not appear to be moral beliefs must either be rejected or they must be found a place under the heading of empirical beliefs. It seems to me that it would have been fairer to the doctrine of the Trinity to reject it than to admit it only in the shape of interpretations that are 'straightforwardly empirical'. In fact, it probably does not matter, from Braithwaite's point of view, what interpretation of the doctrine of the Trinity is adopted. To assign it to the class of empirical assertions is to grant it meaningfulness in itself, but also to exclude it from the range of propositions that essentially express the meaning of religion. If the connection between the moral policy element in religion and the 'stories' is a causal or psychological one, not a logical one, then, as I have already said, it is presumably not necessary to refer to any particular stories in giving an account of the meaning of Christian religious beliefs.

There is something unsatisfactory in another way about the status that Braithwaite provides for his 'stories'. It is not clear on what principle the distinction is to be drawn between the moral beliefs which are at the heart of religion and the stories which attach to them in the thoughts of the believer. Why, for instance, are the doctrine of the Trinity and the doctrine of the Atonement given as instances of accompanying stories rather than as part of the central moral core? The natural answer to this, that they do not directly express anything to do with the adoption of a moral policy, can hardly be given by Braithwaite himself. As we have noted, he makes one of the differences between religious moral assertions and ordinary moral assertions to consist in the fact that the religious assertions form a system. This is clearly to cover the fact that the religious believer does not generally say in so many words that he is adopting a certain moral policy. That this is what he really means would have to be discovered by taking together many things that he says. There will not be one isolable assertion which explicitly says, 'I hereby adopt an agapeistic policy, and this is my central religious assertion'. If there were such an assertion people would not have been ignorant for so many centuries, before Braithwaite illumined the matter, that this is in fact the real meaning of religious assertions. As Braithwaite says:

[I]f a religious assertion is the declaration of an intention to carry out a certain policy, what policy does it specify? The religious statement itself will not explicitly refer to a policy, as does a moral statement; how then can the asserter of the statement know what is the policy concerned, and how can he intend to carry out a policy if he does not know what the policy is? I cannot intend to do something I know not what (p. 80). [Braithwaite's answer is to say that] if a religious assertion is regarded as representative of a large number of assertions of the same religious system, the body of assertions of which the particular one is a representative specimen is taken by the asserter as *implicitly* [my italics] specifying a particular way of life. It is no more necessary for an empiricist philosopher to explain the use of a religious statement taken in isolation from other religious statements than it is for him to give a meaning to a scientific hypothesis in isolation from other scientific hypotheses. We understand scientific hypotheses, and the terms that occur in them, by virtue of the relation of the whole system of hypotheses to empirically observable facts; and it is the whole system of hypotheses, not one hypothesis in isolation, that is tested for its truth-value against experience. So there are good precedents, in the empiricist way of thinking, for considering a system of religious assertions as a whole, and for examining the way in which the whole system is used (pp. 80–1). [He goes on:] If we do this the fact that a system of religious assertions has a moral function can hardly be denied (p. 81).

But what is the system of Christian religious assertions? The notion of a *system* of assertions implies not just a collection of assertions but a collection of interrelated assertions. If we are to be able to talk of a *system* there has to be some relation between the assertions, and probably a relation such that if some members are removed the system is no longer the same system. On any traditional view of the system of Christian belief the Trinity and the Atonement would undoubtedly appear as items. Yet on Braithwaite's account of religious belief it is doubtful whether these are properly members of the system; for he admits them only in the form of 'straightforwardly empirical' interpretations, or 'stories', and stories he has described as having no logical connection with the assertions about adopting an agapeistic policy but only a causal or psychological connection. We are asked to accept a view according to which the central core of religious belief consists in assertions of intention to adopt a certain moral policy, yet we are not to expect to find an explicit assertion of this form; it is rather that we are to interpret this as the real meaning of the whole 'system' of Christian religious assertions, while at the same time the examples Braithwaite gives of what most

Christian thinkers would regard as members of the system of Christian religious assertions are characterised by him in such a way that they seem to be dispensable. We are not told that religious beliefs include a number of items that even a non-believer would have no hesitation in classifying as explicitly moral ('Love thy neighbour as thyself', for example). This would be an entirely plausible thing to say. But Braithwaite prefers to write as if this message had to be somehow by special analysis dug out of the system of religious beliefs, instead of being there perfectly visible on the surface as one item in the system, which is what most commentators on Christianity would say. As he has chosen to make the notion of the *system* of religious belief part of his view it is not unreasonable to expect him to give a fairly full account of the contents of this system as he sees it, especially in view of the surprising exclusions that seem to be implied. If the system exhibits only indirectly the intention to commit oneself to a moral policy, then the fact that the doctrines of the Trinity or of the Atonement do not explicitly state such an intention does not seem to be a good reason for treating them as not part of the system but as merely psychologically associated stories. What would be an example of something that clearly is to be included in the system? And what, more generally, are the criteria for inclusion or exclusion?

It seems to me, as I have indicated already, that the fault lies not so much in Braithwaite's attempting to assimilate religious beliefs to moral. After all, there is a very important moral element in religion, and it is understandable that some should want to say that it is the most important element. The fault lies in Braithwaite's adoption of a narrow view of morality itself; he is forced then to distort religion to make it fit a limited kind of model. As we have noted earlier, the chief virtue that Braithwaite claims for the view of morality that he adopts is that on it there is no gap between moral belief and practical intention. Here is the source of the difficulty. If this gap were allowed to remain in the case of morality, as it does in other moral theories, it might well constitute a problem, but the corresponding gap in the case of religion would be no more of a problem. Because Braithwaite supposes he has solved this problem in the case of morality the corresponding problem in the case of religion seems to him both now to stand alone and to require a solution along similar lines. I have already quoted the passage in which he writes:

Unless a Christian's assertion that God is love (*agape*)—which I take to epitomize the assertions of the Christian religion—be taken to declare his intention to follow an agapeistic way of life, he could be asked what is the connection between the assertion and the intention, between Christian belief and Christian practice. And this question can always be asked if religious assertions are separated from conduct. Unless religious principles are moral principles, it makes no sense to speak of putting them into practice (p. 81).

If the gap has been closed in the one case it seems to him that it must be closed in the other, and closed in the same way. But suppose there just *is* such a gap, in the case both of morality and religion? After all, Braithwaite himself has no hesitation in creating a new kind of gap, one between those religious beliefs (whatever they are) which form part of the 'system' and those, expendable, ones which are merely entertained as stories and whose connection with the system is psychological and not logical. He is clearly not worried by this gap, yet more traditional Christian thinkers, considering the items he places on the 'story' side of the gap, would certainly be worried by it. And *they* might well not be worried by the gap between moral belief and moral practice: that, they might say, is simply a feature of morality. They would not regard as gain a view which closes this gap at the expense of opening up another one somewhere down the middle of the whole complex of religious beliefs. 'What is the connection between the assertion and the intention, between Christian belief and Christian practice?' asks Braithwaite. The only answer that seems to him adequate is one that transforms the assertions into intentions. The more traditional thinker might be content with the answer that the connection is 'causal or psychological'. That answer seems to Braithwaite to be inadequate in this case, but entirely adequate when the question concerns the connection between the doctrine of the Trinity or the Atonement and the central system of Christian religious beliefs. The traditional Christian thinker is likely, I should think, to reverse this judgement. He is unlikely to be as much concerned that the connection between Christian belief and Christian practice should be a logical rather than a psychological one as that the connection between one part of Christian belief and another should be a logical rather than a psychological one.

Braithwaite's account of religious belief brushes aside the metaphysical element in religious belief—more strictly, misclassifies it under the moral and empirical labels. It is also possible to see in his account a stress upon the active side of religion at the expense of the contemplative side. But religion is not only a matter of doing things, however central and important that is. For that matter, neither is morality itself simply a matter of doing things—or, better, a matter of intentions to put certain policies into action. Morality, like religion, is concerned with suffering as well as doing.

Many religious utterances have moral *implications*. This is clearly true of, for example, 'God is our Father'. To accept this assertion, as we have remarked earlier, is to accept that all men are brothers, and this in turn is connected in some way (logically? psychologically?) with certain ways of behaving towards other people. But so do some legal or political or economic utterances have moral implications. To recognise that religious (or legal, etc.) utterances may have moral implications is not to be bound to say that they are moral utterances. Some religious beliefs seem to be moral beliefs, others do not, some seem to have moral implications, others do not. Furthermore, the religious beliefs which either are moral or have moral implications include some which have traditionally been regarded as of central importance in religion. This is not being questioned.

It need hardly be said that to reject Braithwaite's view is not necessarily to reject all views which reduce religious utterances to moral utterances. But his is a view which has attracted a considerable amount of attention.

3. *Religious utterances as poetry*

Some form of a reduction of religious language to poetic language is sometimes met with; and there would certainly seem to be points of contact between on the one hand at least some poets and on the other some writers who set out to express their religious experiences. In both cases there may be a recognition of the difficulty of saying what is to be said in a literal straightforward way. The poet and the mystical writer both aim to interpret experience. The poet is trying to convey a point of view about certain events or situations; there is more than meets the eye. Typically a single event or situation is presented in such a way that it is seen to suggest something wider— a general truth about life or the world. The mystical writer may also seek to set forth general truths on the basis of his particular experience.

The likeness between the poet and the mystic (if we may for convenience use the latter term to refer to the writer who sets down religious experience, though it is properly a term with a narrower meaning than that) can be seen on two levels. In the first place, there are likenesses of a relatively superficial kind to be seen in the way they handle language. Much of the Bible *is* poetry, and much poetry deals with religious themes. There is no particular significance in this. It is the Authorised Version, or other even older English translations, of which we say that it is poetry. Most new translations replace the earlier poetic prose with rather prosaic prose. The Authorised Version is poetry because it was made at a time when (and drew upon earlier versions in which) men handled the English language with imagination and vigour. And the reason why much poetry—like much painting—has had religious themes is again that it has in some ages seemed proper for poetry to have religious themes. There are cultural and historical as well as personal reasons why people write religious poems rather than other sorts of poems. But new translations offer evidence that the Bible in English need not be poetry, and much contemporary English poetry shows that poetry need not be religious. (If we are to refer to the originals the point is strengthened. The Psalms are meant to be poetry. The letters of St Paul are meant to be prose. Yet in English translation in the Authorised Version both contain what we should call poetic passages.) One ought perhaps to qualify the statement that the Authorised Version is poetry. It is prose, but prose with properties that are nowadays thought of as poetic. Is it because prose style has deteriorated more than poetry that people are inclined, in order to indicate that a piece of writing shows a feeling for language, to call it poetic?

Some likenesses between poetry and mystical writing, then, are relatively superficial. At a deeper level, however, there is the likeness that I have referred to as consisting in the fact that the poet and the mystic are both wanting to put an interpretation upon experience. They want to bring out a particular significance of their experience. This has little to do with the sort of language they use, in the sense of what kind of words or phrases. Metaphor and analogy may come readily to the pen of the poet or the mystic, but so may they to that of the prose writer on military strategy or natural history.

What one understands reduction of religious language to poetry to be depends upon how one regards poetry, and there are different kinds of poetry. Religious poetry, in the sense of poetry with an explicitly religious theme—like poems in the form of prayers to God—we can presumably rule out. To say that religious language can be reduced to religious poetry makes a less useful statement than that religious language can be reduced to secular poetry, or to poetry unqualified.

One intention in the suggestion that religious utterances are poetry might be that religious utterances need not be taken with too much seriousness. Poetry is understood to be a leisure-time activity—both the writing of it and the reading of it. Life for some might be poorer without it, but their life could go on. Poets may utter 'truths' but those truths can equally well be uttered by somebody else. The thoughts that poets have are seldom unique. It may be a case of what was ne'er so well expressed; but it is also a case of what oft was thought. If we must put up with having the same thoughts expressed badly then we must put up with it. The thoughts, whether well or ill put, are a gloss upon life and by most people not needed for the living of it. But religion, in the traditional view, is not a gloss upon life. Religious beliefs, if taken seriously, should affect a man's whole way of life. Indeed, if his way of life is not affected by his alleged religious beliefs we should doubt whether he did sincerely hold the religious beliefs he claims to hold or whether he really understood them and their implications. The effect of reducing religion to poetry is thus very different from that of reducing it to morality. To regard religious beliefs as reducible to moral beliefs is not to take them less seriously. To regard them as poetry is—at least, as far as the opinion of most people is concerned.

I do not mean to deny the importance of some of what some poets say. But its importance does not spring from its being said by poets. It is important for other reasons; perhaps, indeed, for what might be said to be religious reasons. A notice by a cliff edge headed 'Danger' will generally be saying something important, but this importance does not lie in the materials of which the notice is made, the fact that the letters of the word 'danger' are in red rather than in blue or in black, or in the fact that it was placed there by order of the local council. Its importance lies in its being a warning—of crumbling rock or the like. Similarly, a poet might call attention in a poem to the evanescence of political power, but the interest or importance of this message does not depend upon the fact that he and not another poet wrote the poem, or on its appearing in a certain publication rather than a different one, or on its being a poem at all rather than a piece of prose. (There are, of course, different kinds of importance. I am not thinking here of such notions as that of importance as a stage in the development of a particular writer's style or thought.) It is what is said, in relation to a given context, rather than who says it or how he says it, that matters. This is the case also with religion: what is there said about the existence of God, God's attributes and his relation to man, man's destiny, and the like, is, if true, important. On the crudest level, whether we are going to rejoice in heaven or roast in hell ought to be a matter of importance to us. And this, in a vital sense, is what religion is *about*. These are central themes of (the Christian) religion and they are not central themes of anything else. It is not the case that there are central themes of poetry which are not the themes of anything else. And it is not the case that where a poet happens to deal with themes—which may be religious themes—that are important, that this importance is conferred upon them by the fact that he, the poet, has chosen to deal with them. The central themes of religion are essentially important. The themes of poetry are accidentally of importance. For this reason religious beliefs cannot be fully described as poetic utterances. The reduction of religious beliefs to poetic utterances can be achieved only at the expense of denying to religious beliefs a property they have always traditionally been claimed to have, and to have because they are religious—namely, real importance.

If someone is prepared to pay the price, the reduction can, of course, be made. But it is important to see that the reduction of religious beliefs to the status of poetry amounts to a kind of trivialisation of religious beliefs, and that this constitutes a difference between this kind of reduction and the reduction of them to moral beliefs. It would be difficult to maintain that religious beliefs, *if true*, are unimportant.

Naturally, the view which would reject a total reduction of religious beliefs to poetry need not deny likenesses between religious beliefs and poetry. Indeed, a consideration of likenesses between art in general and religion can be illuminating—particularly a consideration of the place of symbolism in art and in religion. I offer some very brief remarks on religious symbolism in the following, final, section of the chapter.

4. *Religious symbolism*

As well as verbal symbolism religion, unlike poetry, also possesses non-verbal symbolism—crucifixes, the vestments of priests, etc. It is reasonable to suppose that there is a continuity between the verbal and the non-verbal symbols of religion. Crucifixes and priestly vestments take their place in a wider process of expressing 'religious truth'. They would seem to need to be interpreted, as do the analogies used of God in religious verbal utterances. Because both the non-verbal and the verbal symbols are religious symbols they may be presumed to be interpretable in the same way, as conveying the same message, etc. It may be, then, that light can be thrown upon at least some of the verbal symbolism of religion if it is set alongside non-verbal religious symbolism rather than alongside the verbal symbolism of, say, poetry.

Because the symbol is seen to be in a sense nothing in itself, but to have value only in that it stands for something beyond itself, it distances the religious worshipper from God. But because it is typically down-to-earth, 'concrete', 'finite' (lit candles on an altar, for example), it can also induce a feeling of closeness to God which meditating on the abstract notion of God may not achieve.

We cannot know that symbols are symbols unless we recognise that they 'stand for' something else. It is perhaps natural to suppose that we therefore must be able to say not only that they stand for something else but also what it is that they stand for—that is, to suppose that it must be possible to give an account in non-symbolic terms of the object of symbolism. Yet if an adequate

account could be given in non-symbolic terms what would be the
point of giving an account in symbolic terms? It might, of course,
have an expository point, or in the case of non-verbal symbolism
some related kind of attention-gaining point; as a preacher or
politician might introduce an anecdote into a sermon or speech
in order to keep the attention of his audience. But in such cases the
symbolism is not essential to what is being said, and it can be said
without it. In the case of poetry, or non-verbal art, the connection
of what is being said or shown with the way in which it is being
said or shown is not merely accidental. And traditionally this is
what has been maintained about at any rate the verbal symbolism
of religion. Some of what is said about God involves the use of
terms which are not to be understood literally; yet without the use
of these terms, or others like them, it has traditionally been held
that some things cannot be said about God at all.

4

CHRISTIAN THEISM: FOR AND AGAINST

1. *The Ontological Argument*

The case for theism has sometimes been thought to rest on the three traditional theistic 'proofs', the Ontological Argument, the Cosmological Argument, and the Argument from Design—arguments which have shown a remarkable persistence. Their attractions must lie partly in their neatness and brevity—or at any rate in the possibility of their being expressed neatly and briefly. The Argument from Design probably calls for more diffuse expression, but the Ontological Argument and the Cosmological Argument set standards of elegance that have proved a comfort to their defenders and a stimulus to their critics. (I have discussed these theistic proofs more fully elsewhere; see McPherson [1], Chapters 4–6, and [3].) Let us consider first the Ontological Argument.

St Anselm, in Chapter II of the *Proslogion*, addresses God as 'something than which nothing greater can be conceived' (see, e.g. Hick and McGill, p. 4). Let us suppose that God exists merely in the understanding (that is to say, there is an idea of God in the minds of some men), and not also in reality. But then 'God' would not be 'something than which nothing greater can be conceived'; for to exist in reality as well as in the understanding is greater than to exist in the understanding alone. There is a contradiction involved in holding both that 'God' means 'something than which nothing greater can be conceived' and that God exists merely in the understanding. If we take seriously the notion of God as something than which nothing greater can be conceived we see that God must exist; that is, that God must exist 'in reality' and not merely as an idea in the minds of men.

The Ontological Argument attempts to show that God exists

from an examination of the idea of God. ('God's essence involves his existence.') Critics of the Argument, accordingly, have either questioned the idea of God that appears to be stated in the Argument, or they have questioned the logic of an attempt to move from the idea of God to God's existence in reality (or, of course, they have questioned both).

As far as the former point is concerned two kinds of difficulty arise. Neither of them applies to Anselm to the extent that it applies to some other proponents of the Ontological Argument, in particular, Descartes. The first kind of difficulty concerns the possibility of self-contradiction in the idea of God; the second concerns the question whether the notion of necessary existence makes sense.

First: accounts of the nature of God mention such divine attributes as love, mercy, justice, impassibility. *Prima facie*, some of these attributes are not mutually compatible. Perhaps they can be made compatible if they are limited in some way; but, then, what is supposed to be being provided here is an account of God, not of some finite limited being: God must be said to possess the attributes he possesses in perfection. But is perfect justice compatible with perfect mercy; perfect love with perfect impassibility? If the idea of God on which the Argument is based does indeed in this way contain incompatibilities, then the Argument has an insecure basis. (Anselm himself argues later in the *Proslogion* that such apparent incompatibilities can be resolved.)

The second difficulty is a more serious variation on the first. The notion of God as 'something than which nothing greater can be conceived' seems to lead on to the notion of a necessary being; indeed, Anselm says a little later, addressing God, 'You cannot be thought not to be'. Whether or not the notion of necessary existence is contained in the idea of God from which the Argument starts, it certainly plays a part in the Argument itself and as a whole. To the extent that the notion of a necessary being (or of necessary existence) has been in more recent times widely held to be a meaningless one, we have, again, a difficulty for the Ontological Argument.

I have already remarked that Anselm's original version of the Ontological Argument is less open to attack than later ones like that of Descartes. Anselm's initial account of God is presented in very general terms. He does not list the divine attributes. His eventual account of the nature of God is a full one, but it is reserved for the later chapters of the *Proslogion*, after he considers that he has settled, by the Ontological Argument, the question of the existence of God. It appears that Anselm has been careful not to seem to claim knowledge of the nature of God as a basis for the proof of God's existence. As did Aquinas later, he separates the bare question of the existence

of God from questions about the nature of God, and does not attempt
to make the proof of the existence of God depend upon elements in
the nature of God.

It might be said that although Anselm does not mention any
divine attributes in his initial account of the idea of God, nevertheless
these attributes are *implied*. 'You are something than which nothing
greater can be conceived.' This set of words seems to call for some
completion. Nothing greater in respect of what? Anselm's *Proslogion*
was intended for his fellow-believers, who would have been in no
doubt how to interpret his definition of 'God' in terms of specific
divine attributes. Nevertheless, Anselm himself makes no mention
of divine attributes at the beginning of his presentation of the Ontological Argument. He begins from the idea of God reduced to its
barest skeleton. The putting of flesh on these bones is to come later,
after he has satisfied himself that the *existence* of God has been
proved. Reference to the *nature* of God is not needed as a foundation
for the proof of the existence of God: at any rate we may suppose
from the way in which he goes about the development of his Argument that this is what Anselm intended; and the fact, which I have
no wish to deny, that divine attributes are *implied* in his skeletal statement of the idea of God is a fact about the context in which Anselm's
Argument was written and read (and, indeed, is still read)—it is
not necessary to the logic of the Argument itself, if I have understood
Anselm correctly. Anselm's argument rests on the principle of
contradiction. It is not specific attributes of God that we are to appeal
to in the proof of God. It is rather the contradiction that would be
involved in God's being both something than which nothing greater
can be conceived and at the same time not something than which
nothing greater can be conceived.

The second of the difficulties mentioned above concerned the
question whether the notion of necessary existence makes sense.
We can here take together the notion of necessary existence and that
of a necessary being. By 'necessary being' has sometimes been understood 'being whose non-existence implies a contradiction' (Hume
[2], Part IX). Such a view expresses in terms of being or existence
the Leibnizian doctrine that a necessary proposition is one whose
contradictory is self-contradictory. Necessary existence, *so understood*, has been widely taken to be a meaningless notion. I do not
think that Anselm had *this* notion in mind, or that there is any need
to read it into him. What he had in mind was rather something like
'being without beginning or end'; and this is what he meant by his
words, addressed to God, 'You cannot be thought not to be'. The
notion of a being without beginning or end is not an obviously
absurd one. For a valuable discussion of the notion of necessary

E

being see Dr Anthony Kenny's essay 'God and Necessity' (in Williams and Montefiore, pp. 131–51). Kenny offers an account of necessary being as eternal being—an account which is intended to be close to medieval Aristotelian thought. 'God exists', he suggests, if it is a necessary proposition, is so in the sense that if it is true then it always has been true and always will be true (Williams and Montefiore, p. 148). However, as Kenny points out, it is not only God that has been held to be eternal. 'When Aristotelians stated that the heavenly bodies were eternal, and when Lucretius claimed everlasting existence for his atoms, they asserted propositions which by our criterion were necessary.' The eternity of God seems close to what Anselm meant. But it is not Anselm that Kenny is defending; and Anselm, who would certainly have wanted to insist on the uniqueness of God—as the *only* being to whom one could truly say 'You cannot be thought not to be'—would have had to deny that 'eternal' can properly be predicated of anything other than God. At any rate, the notion of necessary being is one that is capable of being understood in more than one way; in particular, someone who uses this notion is not committed to meaning by it the kind of thing that Hume and Kant, and others since, have rejected as absurd; and it seems clear that Anselm did not.

So far we have been commenting on one of the two main lines of criticism of the Ontological Argument mentioned at the beginning; that is, the criticism that the idea of God, on which the Argument is based, is absurd or meaningless. Let us now turn to the other line of criticism. This concerned the difficulty involved in attempting to move from the 'mere' idea of God to the 'real' existence of God. Anselm himself arrived at the Ontological Argument as a result of dissatisfaction with the kind of argument to God he had earlier offered in his own *Monologion*—an argument both complex and based on consideration of existing things. By contrast, the argument of the *Proslogion* is intended by him to be both simple and abstract, or *a priori*. But it is its *a priori* character that critics have often found objectionable, and some critics have preferred the approach which Anselm himself thought it proper to reject: they have claimed that it is only from existence that existence can be proved; that an argument to God must find a more solid foundation than the mere *idea* of God, a foundation, namely, in the *existence* of (created) things. They have wanted, that is, to develop a version of the Cosmological Argument.

To attempt to draw out existence from a bare idea would seem a quite misconceived enterprise. With this Anselm himself might largely agree. There is no suggestion in Anselm that from the mere idea of any created thing one could argue to its existence. Indeed, his reply on this point to the suggestion of Gaunilo that if Anselm were right we ought to be able to define the most perfect island into existence, though rather unsatisfactorily brief, makes it clear that the Ontological Argument is only supposed to work in the case of God (for Gaunilo's criticisms and Anselm's replies see Hick and McGill). The idea of God is not the idea of that thing which is greatest of any kind—like the greatest (most perfect) island. (God is in any case not a thing—an entity among entities—and God is not a member of any kind.) God is not that x (say, that god) than which no greater x can be conceived; God is that than which no greater can be conceived. The idea of God is supposed by Anselm to be a unique idea; it is only from this one idea and not from any other that he supposes existence can be deduced. We are told that 'God' means 'that (or something) than which . . .'; but are we not bound to ask 'That *what* than which . . .?'? But the point to note here is that it is not an adequate reaction to Anselm simply to say, 'But how can one argue from ideas to reality?' Anselm does not suppose that one can do this—in general. The case of the idea of God, he would claim, is unique. This is not to say that he is *correct* in thinking that one can argue from idea to reality in the single case of the idea of God. That a reasonably adequate conception of God, even though this may fall short of a full understanding (and Anselm does not suppose that we can have a full understanding of the concept of God), must include the conception of God as existing is one thing; that God exists 'in reality' is another.

It has been maintained—as by Kant—that proponents of the Ontological Argument may suppose that they have proved a necessary being when all they have done, or could do, is to produce an instance of logical necessity. Anselm's argument depends, as we saw, upon the principle of contradiction. We should be contradicting ourselves, he maintains, if we first defined 'God' in a certain way and then went on to deny God's existence. 'God' is 'something than which nothing greater can be conceived'. In order to see that God must exist all we need to do is attend closely to this expression, 'something than which nothing greater can be conceived'. However, in saying that God must exist, all that we could really mean, the critic claims, is that the conclusion of our argument is necessitated by its premises together with the rules of logic. 'God must exist' is elliptical for 'It must be the case that God exists', and says nothing about a special *kind* of existence (necessary existence) possessed by God.

But this does not, I think, constitute a difficulty for Anselm. If the conclusion 'God exists' follows from the premises (supposing it does) what more could Anselm want? It is true that he says, as we noted, 'You cannot be thought not to be'; but, as I have remarked already, he (at any rate) did not intend this to be interpreted as meaning that God possesses necessary existence in the sense that Hume and Kant were to reject. Anselm claimed that there would be a contradiction involved in defining 'God' in the way he does and then denying God's existence, but not that God possesses a special kind of existence such that its denial would be self-contradictory rather than false.

It has already been noted that Anselm's argument is one intended for his fellow-believers rather than one meant to convince non-believers. In the *Proslogion*, the argument is preceded by a chapter in which Anselm says in a famous sentence, 'I do not seek to understand in order that I may believe, but I believe in order that I may understand'. Anselm begins, then, with a belief in the existence of God. It would appear from this that his argument is defensible against a certain criticism sometimes made. It has been said by some critics that if we already knew that God as a matter of fact existed, the Ontological Argument might provide some reason for saying that he *must* exist; but that it cannot of itself show the existence of God. The assumptions here are that proponents of the Ontological Argument, such as Anselm, have intended it as an argument to prove the existence of God to people who do not already believe in God, and that if it fails to do this, it can be written off. This, however, is to ignore the context in which Anselm, the inventor of the Argument, set it. 'For this also I believe, that unless I believe I shall not understand.' The purpose of the Argument was to assist to a fuller understanding of God those who were already believers in God and who did not need to be argued into believing in the existence of God. The sense in which the Argument might assist a believer's understanding would seem to be that it makes plain to him that God has neither beginning nor end. We may have in Anselm, then, an instance of a kind of argument that some critics have conceded could be taken seriously. We must have, according to Anselm, independent conviction of the existence of God. The force of the Argument itself is to help to bring out what it is that one is believing in if one believes in divine existence.

2. *The Cosmological Argument*

I shall take the Third Way of St Thomas Aquinas as representative of the Cosmological Argument. Aquinas argues in the following manner. Some things we encounter come into being and pass away again. But it is impossible that everything should be of this kind: for if that were the case then there must have been a time when nothing existed at all; there would be nothing that could bring about the existence of anything else; and so nothing could ever begin to exist, and there would be nothing now. But clearly things do exist. So it must be a mistake to suppose that everything that exists is of the kind that has a beginning and an end. There must exist also necessary beings or a necessary being. Some necessary beings have their cause outside themselves, but there cannot be an infinite series of such necessary beings. There must be a necessary being which has no cause of its necessity outside itself. And this all men call God. (*Summa Theologica*, I, 2, 3; for interpretations of the Third Way see Kenny, also Durrant [1].)

One difficulty presents itself at once. Granted that the contingent things of our everyday experience—and, indeed, we ourselves— have a beginning and an end, it does not follow, as Aquinas seems to be suggesting, that there would have been a time at which no contingent things existed at all (and, as he says, therefore a time at which *nothing* existed at all, if contingent things are the only things there are). If we take the most natural interpretation of this—namely, one in temporal terms—there would seem to be no reason why things should not always temporally overlap, so that although any given thing will indeed come to an end, at least a great many contingently existing things will not do so until they have been instrumental in bringing about the existence of other things, which will outlast them and in their turn will not pass out of existence without bringing about yet other things. Thus, although when we go back in time we will certainly go back before the beginning of any given thing, it need not be the case that we will go back before the beginning of everything. It may be the case, for all we are entitled to conclude from the mere fact that every particular contingent thing has a beginning in time, that there is an infinite temporal regress of con- tingent things. (Aquinas, as far as the Five Ways are concerned, is not necessarily asserting that the world could not have existed from eternity (see Copleston, p. 120), but, as Kenny reminds us, he did in fact believe that the world was *created*. Aquinas may have intended to say not that if everything that exists is contingent there must have been a time when there was nothing, but that in that case there will be a time when there will be nothing (see Kenny, Chapter IV, especially pp. 50–1, 57–8, 63–4.)

We should note that it is possible to interpret the reference to a regress in Aquinas' argument as being a reference not to a temporal regress but to a regress of another kind. What Aquinas is asserting may be the impossibility of an infinite regress of *dependence*. He is saying that if everything is dependent for its existence on something else there is no sufficient reason why anything should exist at all. Things 'cannot account for their own occurrence', as Professor

E. L. Mascall has put it (Mascall, p. 85). In order for there to be contingent things at all—and we know that there are contingent things—there must be necessary beings or a necessary being.

There are three classes of persons the effect on whom of the Cosmological Argument we shall now consider.

First, there is the non-religious man. The Argument assumes a view of the world which he is unlikely to share. How, indeed, could he share it; for it is a religious view of the world, and he is a non-religious man? The argument attempts to show how reflection on the finite, contingent, or incomplete character of the world can lead to the conclusion that behind the world, accounting for its existence, is the infinite, the necessary, the complete. But this is a line of thought that he cannot agree to, and perhaps cannot even understand; for he does not share the view of the world as limited or incomplete. Certainly, in the sense in which the theist understands such notions, the non-theist does not share them. Things are as they are. That they are limited in time and space need not create a problem for him requiring a theistic or any other solution.

This is perhaps to put the point over-strongly. Kant's First Antinomy (that the world has a beginning in time and is limited in space and yet that it has no beginning in time and no limits in space) might worry someone who is not disposed to theism. So might the question 'Why is there anything at all?' It would be wrong to suggest that everyone troubled by metaphysical questions must be already halfway to theism. Perhaps some theists have supposed this; but it seems a large supposition. The non-theist who is also a non-metaphysician, who is not concerned about large questions of the finite and the infinite, will not follow the Cosmological Argument, for it makes assumptions about the world which he simply does not share. It might be retorted that we do not need to take seriously the limitations of the insensitive or the unphilosophical. Mathematical problems exist for mathematicians even though the non-mathematical may not see them as problems. Must we say that Bach's *Mass in B Minor* is not great music because the unmusical may not appreciate it? But it is not simply a matter of failure to see significances that can be seen by others more sensitive or better trained. We are not concerned with the contrast between the mathematically minded and the innumerate, between people of musical sensibility and musical clods. The contrast is more like that between lovers of the exclusively classical and lovers of the exclusively romantic in music. The non-religious man I am imagining here is not an unthinking man; he is a man who thinks about the world in a way other than that in which the theist does. The theist may try to persuade him to think like him. But the Cosmological Argument, which is what we are considering, does not so much constitute persuasion to a certain point of view about the world as assume that point of view.

The second category of persons to be considered is that of religious non-theists (as opposed to non-believers). The religious non-theist is prepared to look upon the world as limited or incomplete, upon life as (in a meaningful way) transient, etc. This may suggest to him something 'beyond' or 'behind' it all. But this something does not take for him a theistic form. Theism is not the only possibility for someone disposed to religious belief; or at any rate theism of the traditional Christian kind is not the only possibility. Consider, for instance, nature mysticism; or contemporary Western interest in some forms of Hinduism and Buddhism, both of which are largely non-theistic. It is clearly possible for a person to take what may be called a religious attitude to the world while not considering that he is bound to let this attitude crystallise in theistic form. In order for the Cosmological Argument to be an effective argument in support of theism it would have to be the case that the conclusion of the Argument was capable only of a theistic interpretation—that and no other. But this is not the case. The conclusion is to necessary being or necessary beings; and the notion of necessary being (or that of necessary existence) is capable of being interpreted in non-theistic terms—as, for instance, by Spinoza, for all that he uses the term 'God'. The remark with which the Third Way ends (and Aquinas repeats more or less the same form of words at the end of all the Five Ways) is 'And this all men call God'. This has been well described as a 'sociological' remark. What is arrived at in the conclusion of the Cosmological Argument can be said to be (or to be part of) that which theists have in mind when they talk of God, but just as there is no suggestion in Aquinas that the Argument exhausts the meaning of 'God' (rather the opposite), so we may say that there is nothing that would preclude someone's making a different identification—nothing, say, to prevent someone's adopting Aquinas' argument but ending it not with 'And this all men call God' but with, for example, 'And this I understand to be mind or spirit'. The concluding remark in the statement of the Argument is a remark *about* the true conclusion of the Argument, which is that a self-explanatory necessary being exists. There would be nothing inconsistent in someone's saying that he accepted Aquinas' argument as valid but nevertheless did not adopt on his own account the concluding sociological remark 'And this all men call God'. *He* might prefer to speak of it otherwise. (Of course, given its context, the tradition of Christian natural theology, Aquinas' is a correct sociological remark to make about the Cosmological Argument.)

We turn to the third category of persons—theistic believers. For

such believers, assuming they accept and use the Cosmological
Argument, the Argument is hardly an argument at all, but rather a
way of bringing out what is involved in their belief. Compare what
was said above about Anselm. The kind of sense that the believer
(if he used this language) would give to the world's 'finiteness', its
'contingent' character, its 'incompleteness', etc., is such that the
notion of God (God the Creator, etc.) is already assumed. It is only
someone who already believed in God who would be likely to look
upon the world in that way.

To sum up. From the point of view of the non-religious person,
the Cosmological Argument assumes a view of the world which he
does not share, a view which is only one among several possible
ways of looking at the world, and the Argument itself offers no
reasons why the view of the world which it assumes is to be preferred
to any other one. Of course, like all arguments, it is hypothetical:
'*If* the world is incomplete, etc. . . .' As far as its logic is concerned
it might therefore be claimed that its validity is in no way dependent
on whether anyone happens to accept its premiss. But I am concerned
at present with how far the argument is likely to appear cogent to
those who hear or read it. In any case, as we shall shortly see, a
kind of circularity may well be involved.

From the point of view of the religious person who is not attracted
by theism, the Argument, once again, does not succeed in achieving
what it sets out to achieve. The religious non-theist can share the
attitude to the world from which the Cosmological Argument starts.
He can even perhaps share its conclusion. But he does not share the
theist's interpretation of that conclusion.

From the point of view of the theist himself the Argument may be
said to be too good to be true. The sense which the theist gives to the
notion of the limited or incomplete character of the world is such
as to assume a theistic conclusion. He is not arguing to God so much
as bringing out what is involved in the correlative beliefs in the
finiteness of the world and the infiniteness of God. In order to be
able to conclude to *God* from a premiss about the finiteness of the
world. that premiss has to be understood in a way determined by
the conclusion that it is intended should eventually be drawn.
Merely that the world is finite or limited does not necessitate God;
for, as we have remarked already, there can be non-theistic con-
clusions from such a premiss. It can seem to necessitate it if the
finiteness of the world is understood as needing completion in the
sort of way the theist assumes, that is, in terms of the creating and
sustaining God. Hence the circularity mentioned above. As far as
its practical effect is concerned, the Cosmological Argument will
seem to lead to a theistic conclusion for someone who is already a theist.

This is a fault if one believes, as Aquinas himself believed, that the Cosmological Argument should help to convince non-believers; and more particularly if one believes that if it fails in this then it has no further value. However, as I have already said in the case of Anselm, the failure of the theistic 'proofs' to convince the non-believer need not be taken as an adequate reason for discarding them; for their function might be regarded as that of making clearer to the theistic believer the nature of his own belief, or of convincing him of something that he is disposed to believe in any case. To quote Anselm again: '*Unless* I believe I shall not understand'. This certainly does not, as far as I can see, reduce the importance of the so-called theistic 'proofs' for theistic religion. 'No-one was ever argued into theism.' Perhaps; though this is surely not entirely true: but this does not mean that the so-called theistic arguments are of no value, for their religious value may lie elsewhere than in their character as 'proofs' of the existence of God.

3. *The Argument from Design*

From the order and design observable in the universe we may conclude—so the Argument from Design runs—that there is a supreme orderer or designer. The kind of Argument from Design that I propose to consider enjoyed its heyday in the eighteenth and nineteenth centuries. It is an argument in which analogies are developed between specific parts of nature (for example, the human eye, or the solar system) and machines made by man, and in which it is maintained that just as machines give evidence of having been designed by a human mind so parts of the universe—or, it may be, the universe as a whole—give evidence of having been designed by a mind greater than human: a cosmic designer or supreme architect.

Hume, in his critical discussion of the Argument from Design (see Hume [2]), calls attention to the uniqueness of the universe. Arguments by analogy, he says, are only possible where we have *species* of things: where we are able to argue that because C resembles A and B in certain respects it probably resembles them in other respects also. But we are not able to compare the universe with other universes. It is not as if we had knowledge in the case of some other universes that they were the creation of a divine designer and could then argue that as our own universe resembles these others in various significant respects it probably also resembles them in being the work of a divine designer. No such comparison is possible; for there are no other universes. By definition *the* universe is 'unique and unparalleled'. Thus, the Argument from Design, though it purports to be an argument by analogy, cannot be an argument by analogy.

If Hume were right there would presumably be no need to describe in detail analogies between the universe and machines: we should know from the outset that argument by analogy was impossible in this case. This only needs to be stated, however, for a weakness in Hume's position to appear. Certainly, the universe is unique; but—this is the important thing—it is not indescribable. The universe in the sense of an assemblage of physical bodies—the stars, the planets, etc. (which is the sense of 'universe' that Hume himself had in mind in the *Dialogues*)—is the subject of scientific description and speculation; its 'uniqueness' has certainly not proved an insuperable obstacle to scientific work. Scientists have been able to speculate upon, among other things, its origins, and have not been hampered in this by the fact that they have been unable to compare this universe with others whose origins were known (see Swinburne, p. 208). Of course, it might be said that scientists who speculate about the origin of the universe are not reasoning by analogy, and that therefore this is not an appropriate answer to Hume's specific point. But Hume was much influenced by Newton, and may be presumed to have shared with him the view that scientific argument is argument by analogy. A main question running through Hume's *Dialogues* is the question of whether the Argument from Design is or is not a kind of scientific argument. Its seeming plausibility, Hume thought, sprang from its appearance of being a quasi-scientific argument, and he was concerned to question this appearance. (See Swinburne; McPherson [3], Chapter 5.) In his view the Argument was not scientifically respectable, and this is the point of his attempt to show that it is not a genuine argument by analogy. If it is not an argument by analogy then, from the point of view that Hume shared, it is not a scientific or quasi-scientific argument. Thus at once it loses the force it seemed to have for people who were at the same time theists and also immersed in the new developments in science—people like Newton himself. It is not, then, irrelevant to comment on Hume by pointing out that scientists do in fact speculate upon the origins of the universe, etc., and are not prevented from doing this by the 'uniqueness' of the universe.

In any case, it is not clear that Arguments from Design are bound to argue, as Hume supposes, from the universe as a whole. They must in some sense argue *to* the universe as a whole; but the drawing of analogies can be done on a more limited level. Particular aspects of the universe (for example, the human eye or the solar system, to take again examples already mentioned) rather than the universe as a whole may suggest to a proponent of the Argument likenesses to machines and thus the possibility of their having a designer as machines have a designer. Even if a proponent of the Argument does find himself arguing from the universe as a whole he does not need, in order to be able to argue analogically, to invoke non-existent other universes. The analogies he draws will be between the universe and machines, not between the universe and other universes.

Let us now leave the matter of the 'uniqueness' of the universe and consider another point made by Hume, namely, his dictum that from finite effects it is possible to argue only to finite causes, or that from a given effect it is possible to argue only to a cause great enough to produce just that effect but no greater. As the Argument from Desigy is supposed to be an argument based upon evidence, it is clearly limited by the limitations of the evidence. Evidence of order or design in the universe may point to a superhuman orderer or designer; but it cannot justify a conclusion to the infinite God. Hume was not alone in noting a tendency on the part of proponents of the Argument to think that by its use they could prove the existence of something like the Christian God.

Hume is right in his main contention here. Supposing the Argument from Design to prove anything at all it certainly does not prove the infinite God. The proponent of the theistic arguments, if he wants to put forward the Argument from Design as a proof of God, will have to be content with a finite God—perhaps a demiurge, perhaps not a creator even in a limited sense but only a designer using material that he finds already in existence. No stronger conclusion than this can be made to follow from the line of reasoning of a typical Argument from Design; at any rate, if it is taken alone.

The three theistic arguments we are considering here have, however, frequently been offered not as alternatives to each other but as supplementary to or supportive of each other, no doubt in the belief that deficiencies in one may be made up for by strengths in another. If they could be credibly harnessed together the resulting complex argument would on the face of it seem likely to be stronger than any one of them could be on its own. In particular, bearing in mind the present difficulty in the case of the Argument from Design, the Ontological Argument and the Cosmological Argument seem to offer that very conclusion to the *infinite* God that the Argument from Design, unaided, can never reach. (I am writing throughout, for simplicity, of 'the' Argument from Design, 'the' Ontological Argument, 'the' Cosmological Argument; but it needs to be said that there are different versions of all these arguments. A combination of 'the' three Arguments would amount to something rather different depending on what versions of each were involved.)

It has been argued by Kant that the Argument from Design and the Cosmological Argument both must fall back upon the Onto-logical Argument (Kant, pp. 507–24); which means that if the

Ontological Argument can be refuted, the other two arguments would fall with it. As the Argument from Design can lead only to a conclusion in terms of something finite—a designer, but only a super-human designer, not an infinite creator and designer—to get a stronger conclusion we must move on from the Argument from Design and follow through the reasoning of the Cosmological Argument based upon the contingency of the world. But even this would not be enough. What the Cosmological Argument provides is the idea of a necessary being. To get from this to a real infinite being we should need finally to go on to the Ontological Argument (God's existence follows from his nature); and as this is invalid— according to Kant, chiefly for the reasons that it involves treating existence as a real predicate and that it depends upon a confusion between logical necessity and necessary existence—the whole enterprise fails.

I do not propose to discuss the question whether this Kantian argument (which in any case is here represented in very crude terms) is correct. I wish, however, to make two comments. First, provided the proponent of the Argument from Design were content with a finite god then he need not submit to persuasion to combine the Argument from Design with the other two Arguments and thus, if Kant is right, weaken it by making the objections to them also objections to it. (When proponents of the theistic arguments have wanted to put forward several arguments together they have done so, naturally enough, in the belief that each would help to strengthen, not weaken, the others.) However, I do not think that the Argument has often been put forward as a proof of God by people who both acknowledged that it could at the most prove only a finite god and who were content with this. Secondly, to return to a point I have been making throughout this chapter, all the theistic arguments, and therefore the Argument from Design, appear in a rather different light if we see their function as one of serving to make more explicit the faith of people who are already theists rather than, as Kant among many others has assumed, as serving to convince even non-theists of the existence of God. Even if the arguments proved nothing at all they would not necessarily be worthless to the person who is already a theistic believer: they can function as trains of thought which have the effect of making clearer to him some aspects of what he believes anyway. The most explicit expression of this point of view that is known to me is that of William Paley, who at the end of his presentation of the Argument from Design, which takes up the whole of his quite lengthy *Natural Theology* (1802), asks why his readers, who may be presumed to be already believers in God, should need to read a work which apparently only tells them what they know already. Paley answers that the use of such a book as his is partly that it offers arguments in support of what its readers may have so far believed only upon authority, and thus provides their beliefs with a firm basis (so far this is compatible with the view of the Argument which sees it purely as an attempt to *prove* the existence of God); but also partly its use lies in its moral and religious value in helping its readers to acquire a certain habit of thought, an attitude to the world in which the world becomes a temple 'and life itself one continued act of adoration'. In this latter use the Argument can have a value for the religious believer independent of whether it is a valid proof of the existence of God. Its value would lie in helping to build a religious attitude. Of course, the Argument itself offers no justification of the taking up of a religious attitude to someone who does not see any virtue in having a religious attitude. But in any case, no doubt, no one could be easily persuaded of the value of a religious attitude unless he already has one or the beginnings of one.

It might be said that arguments can only provide support for beliefs if they are sound. I should, however, say that psychological support for a belief is important (though not 'logically important'). The theistic arguments we have discussed are not logically valid as proofs of the existence of God; and it may well be also that they have not in fact functioned in seeming to provide grounds for the religious beliefs of a very large number of believers, though I think they have probably played a larger part than is sometimes allowed by those who react strongly against traditional natural theology. The Ontological Argument is undeniably not 'popular', but many others than myself must have heard Protestant preachers preaching intelligible sermons which were no more than arguments from design, and auditors of Roman Catholic instruction can hardly fail to be made familiar with cosmological arguments. I should judge that the reflective believer, or half-believer, may well from time to time enter into trains of thought about apparent design in the universe, or about the apparently dependent character of contingent things. The confirming of an already-held belief is in practice not merely a matter of devising or adopting logically watertight arguments in support of it. Of course, if grounds for a belief are to be given at all it is as well if they are (logically) good grounds; but the process of deepening and confirming belief is a complex thing. Psychological grounds for religious belief are neither unimportant nor no concern of philosophers of religion. (See the discussion of Freud in section 5 of the present chapter.)

So far we have been concerned with 'the case for theism'—more strictly, with a limited aspect of this. What is presented as a case for theism may not be a case for theism as this is understood within Christianity. There is a gap to be crossed between the supreme designer and God; and the conclusion of the Cosmological Argument, as we saw, is even capable of interpretation in non-theistic terms. It may be allowed that the Ontological Argument provides a conclusion to a God worthy of Christian worship; but the idea of God which it uses is minimal in content. Even if all these three theistic arguments were arguments to an unequivocally theistic, and Christian theistic, conclusion, they are open to logical objections. But their value for religion, as I have said, can be seen as lying elsewhere. This, no doubt, may present somewhat the air of falling back upon a second-best—as if one were searching about to find something to say in their favour. If their chief value is to 'confirm' already existing faith and to make clearer the notion of God might one not expect it to be declared in these terms by all their inventors and users? There may seem something suspicious in its being produced when they have been seen to fail to prove God: the philosophical theologian is on the point of retiring defeated, when a way of saving the day suddenly occurs to him. . . . But I can only say that the suggestion, as made by Paley at any rate, that the arguments have this role does not seem to me to be mere second thoughts. This was not a main intention of all the inventors of the arguments—it was not an intention of Aquinas, to take the most important case—but it is still a value that they can be properly represented as having for the believer.

A case for theism perhaps might be expected to consist of arguments which a non-believer should find cogent and persuasive and which should go some way towards inducing in him theistic belief. Presenting 'the case for' something normally suggests an attempt to persuade to the acceptance of a certain position someone who may be disposed to reject it or who at best is neutral in his attitude to it. If someone already adheres to a set of beliefs he would not generally need to have presented to him a case for it. But there may be exceptions to this. Paley certainly seems to have thought so. If a person's adherence is weak—for example, because (as Paley said) it is an adherence on grounds of authority rather than of argument, or (as we might say) because he is nervously aware of living in an environment hostile to such adherence—even the believer may be glad to have his beliefs psychologically shored-up by having presented to him 'the case for theism'.

As I have remarked already, what we have been considering is only an aspect of the case for theism. These three are not the only theistic 'proofs' which have been offered; and some would in any case wish to defend theism in ways other than by the offering of arguments of this kind. The most effective critic of these three traditional 'proofs'—Kant—nevertheless himself was prepared to offer rational grounds, of a kind, for belief. His famous remark that he had found it necessary 'to deny *knowledge*, in order to make room for *faith*' (Kant, p. 29) does not indicate a simple replacement of rational grounds for belief in God by 'mere' faith: it is rather a replacement of false claims to knowledge by what has been called 'rational faith'. Kant's position is that although God is not knowable by speculative reason the concept of God is nevertheless a meaningful one, and that acceptance of *the moral law*, which requires that we make ourselves worthy of happiness, demands faith in, or the postulation of, the existence of God (as it does also of freedom and immortality); unless there is God to guarantee a proper connection between virtue and happiness the perfect good is not attainable by rational beings. Kant's views in general have relevance to several of the topics dealt with in this book. As we have just seen, they are clearly relevant to the question whether commitment or faith can be rational (see Chapter 1, section 4). And, on the central Kantian theme of the reconciliation of science—specifically, Newtonian physics—with morality and religion, the view that morality and religion should conform to canons laid down by science (as W. W. Bartley in effect assumes: see the discussion in Chapter 6, section 2, *infra*) was precisely what Kant argued against. (On Kant see Körner, esp. pp. 163–71; and Webb.)

But let us now turn to some aspects of the case against theism.

4. *The problem of evil*

The problem of evil has long presented an obstacle to theistic belief. How can the acknowledgement that there is evil and suffering in the world be reconciled with belief in an all-good and all-powerful God? A solution may seem to lie in limiting God. If God were either not all-good or not all-powerful the problem as it traditionally presents itself would disappear: it cannot arise on the supposition of an all-good but weak deity, or an all-powerful but bad or indifferent deity. But the problem is essentially one for Christian theism, and the Christian theist will naturally resist any suggestion that he might solve it by abandoning Christian theism. That may have to come, but not yet; and those to whom a suggested solution like that just mentioned appears at once an acceptable one have not felt the problem as the Christian theist feels it.

A less Draconian method of limiting the notion of God consists not in denying that he is both all-good and all-powerful but rather in defining the notion of divine goodness or that of divine omnipotence in such a way as to admit of the possibility of evil. Thus: God's goodness is not human goodness; there are reasons why God in his goodness permits what we call evil, but they are not reasons that we can be expected to understand—just as a child may not understand that his father's severity towards him is really motivated by love. Or we might say that God exercises his omnipotence by placing restrictions upon himself; or we might say that even supreme power does not need to be actually exercised all the time. But, again, these milder limitations may not commend themselves to the Christian theist. They rest upon analogies with human behaviour, but with a kind of human behaviour that we are not disposed to think well of, let alone think god-like. A father may discipline his son in his son's best interests, but we should not morally approve of a father who behaved cruelly to his son in his or anyone else's alleged interests, or was apparently indifferent to his son's serious suffering, or failed to take active steps that were within his power to help protect him against suffering. Yet that is how God, it seems, behaves. Similarly, a man who never used his alleged power in the service of the prevention of evil would justly be suspected of not really possessing such power—if we did not suspect him of worse. It might be said that there is much less evil in the world than there could have been: that God already ensures that there exists only a minimum quantity of evil. But there would seem to be no way of establishing that this is so; if we are to talk in these terms it will invite the retort that it certainly looks as if there is even yet more evil than there need have been: for instance, why not just one fewer earthquake every thousand years? Admittedly, speculation of this kind is questionable. There are causes of such things as earthquakes, and the supposition that a given earthquake which has occurred might not have occurred would be difficult to reconcile with the belief that we live in a law-governed universe. It is more meaningful to suppose that the universe as a whole might have been different all along than that it should be much as it is but that particular things in it might be altered, and it is the second of these suppositions that we are considering here. But even if we were prepared to grant it to be not only meaningful, which is doubtful, but true that there is less evil in the world than there might have been, the original problem is not finally disposed of but only shown to be, from a certain point of view, less serious than one might at first have supposed. There are general problems about how we are to understand terms like 'power', 'goodness', 'love' when these are applied to God; but the point I am concerned to make at present is merely that when a stand is taken upon the analogy with loving but severe human fathers, or powerful but inactive human rulers, and the like, then it may be difficult for the theist to ignore some unwelcome aspects of these analogies.

Another way out for the theist might seem to lie in limiting or redefining the notion of evil itself. If evil and suffering were 'unreal' the problem would surely disappear. However, the notion of the unreality of evil is a somewhat refined one. No one suffering from toothache or undergoing torture would willingly agree that his pain was 'unreal'. The sense in which it is unreal, supposing it to be so, must be one in which people can nevertheless still actually suffer pain and evil. Compare views about the unreality of time or of the external world, holders of which do not deny—who could?—that nevertheless in the everyday sense their breakfast preceded their lunch, or that they are sitting at a desk, pen in hand. Even if pain and evil are, in some refined sense, unreal, this is not an answer to the problem of evil, which is caused by the reality, in an everyday sense, of pain and evil; pain and evil in that sense cannot be defined out of existence. In any case, the Christian tradition normally insists upon the 'reality' of pain and evil: otherwise, for instance, the sufferings of Jesus upon the Cross would lose their significance.

But there is another sense of the unreality of pain or evil which is neither the everyday nor a refined sense. Occasionally when things are said to be unreal what is meant is that they are unimportant or comparatively unimportant. Pain or evil may be unreal in the sense that they do not have the significance, or the degree of significance, we tend to give them. It is not that we do not suffer pain; for we do: but we are wrong in dwelling upon it. However, although the problem of evil would in this case no longer *seem* so difficult a problem, it surely still would, or should, *be* a problem for the Christian theist. Some men may become convinced that the importance of pain and evil in life can be exaggerated, but there will always be many who know only that they are suffering severe pain or that they are being extremely badly treated. The theist may for himself be able to reconcile his belief in God with acknowledging the existence of pain and evil, provided he is able to take towards pain and evil the kind of depreciatory attitude just mentioned. But, as this attitude is one that some others do not or cannot share, the problem remains. These others may not themselves feel this as a problem—not being theists, for example, or not being reflective or critical about religious belief—but although the problem arises for the theist and not (or not in the same way) for the non-theist, it is not a problem that the theist can solve purely for his own case. It is not enough that a theist should adopt for himself and his fellow theists a particular minimising or depreciatory attitude towards pain and evil. The test for whether a pain is severe is whether someone considers that the pain he feels is severe; the test for whether an evil is important is whether someone who is actually suffering what he considers ill-treatment, or whatever

F

it may be, considers that the suffering of it is an important ingredient
in his life. Pain and evil are human experiences; and although
individuals may be persuaded, or may persuade themselves, that they
are mistaken in some way in the experiences they think they have,
or are mistaken in assigning to them the degree of importance they
do, the fact that those individuals are so persuaded does not mean
that pain and evil cease to be important. This result could only
follow if *every* human individual came to share the same view. As
long as there is someone somewhere considering pain or evil important then, as far as the theist is concerned, pain or evil must be
acknowledged to be important. It will not do for the theist to say:
'After reflection I am convinced that we all attach too much importance to pain and evil; so the pain you are feeling is not as important as you think it is'. The other can properly reply: 'Speak for
yourself'. Each man's judgement about the importance of (his)
pain, as about its reality, has independent status. Although a theist
may make a claim in the form 'Pain [meaning pain in general] is
not really important' and not in the form 'My pain is not really
important to me', what he says needs to be read in the latter sense,
because of the moral effrontery of one man's presuming to judge
for another in a matter of this kind ('Pain doesn't bother me, so
it shouldn't bother you').

One attempted answer to the problem of evil that has been a good
deal discussed is the 'free will defence'. This consists in maintaining
that the existence of evil in the world is the consequence of God's
having created in men beings with free will. It is possible for them
to choose either good or evil; and this, if it is to be a real choice,
means that sometimes they will choose evil. God might no doubt
have made 'men' so that they lacked free will; but then they would
not have been men at all, and, anyway, he did not. Thus, the existence of evil in the world is at any rate not the direct responsibility
of God; at the most he is indirectly responsible. The existence of
evil is an inseparable consequence of our being the sort of creatures
that we are.

One line of reply to the free will defence takes the form of the
suggestion that the power to choose between good and evil need not
necessarily mean the actual choice of evil on some occasions (see,
e.g. Mackie, reprinted in Mitchell [3], pp. 92–104, and in Pike,
pp. 46–60). For there to be any reality in the doing of good there has
to be a possibility of doing evil. The free will defence claims, and the
counter-argument denies, that there must be actualisation of this
possibility. The counter-argument is suggesting: why may not the
mere idea of doing evil, or the mere temptation to do evil, function
as well as the actual doing of it? Could there not be a real possibility

of doing evil, and therefore a meaningful choice of good, without that possibility's ever being realised? Might we not know what it would be like to do evil although we never did it? (I am considering a generalized version of the counter-argument, not that of any particular writer.) I do not think that the counter-argument succeeds. Pain and evil, as we have already remarked, are parts of human experience; and it is not possible to make someone who has never suffered pain, or has never been the victim of cruel or unjust treatment by someone else, understand what it means to suffer pain or evil. In order for someone to understand for himself what it is to perform or to avoid the performance of evil actions he would have to know what it is to be on the receiving end of such actions, which requires that someone else performs evil actions. And the notion of a temptation to perform evil is parasitic upon the actual performing of evil. The situation here is different from that of someone blind from birth endeavouring to understand the meaning of words which name physical objects. Other senses can take the place of sight, and a blind person can no doubt learn to identify many objects as effectively as a sighted person, and to identify them, in certain respects, in the same way. But the nature of suffering cannot be made plain simply by analogies or through recommending the use of one sense rather than another.

Let us suppose that there are individuals completely without a moral sense, to whom one action is just like another, who make no distinction between good and evil. Such individuals might be taught not to do certain evil actions, in the sense that some of the actions that people with a moral sense regard as evil actions could probably be identified to them by reference to accidental features. Such persons might then refrain from those actions, but not because the actions were evil but at best because they were *called* 'evil' by their teachers and they had learnt to attach that label to them. But it is obviously impossible for morality that *everyone* should be like this. There must be some people who *understand* what evil actions are, who know what it means to perform or avoid actions because they are evil; and what I am claiming is that such understanding requires the actual suffering of evil and hence the actual committing of it. We could of course learn what it is to suffer evil through experience of natural evil; but we could not learn what it is to suffer moral evil unless someone committed moral evil. It is not a requirement for a man's being said to understand moral evil that he should himself commit evil; what is required is that someone else should commit it against him (together with his recognition of certain causal connections). This means that what would otherwise be an objection to the position that I have outlined can be avoided or at least softened—namely, that if it is impossible to choose good unless evil is sometimes chosen then it might be necessary to say that *God* must sometimes do evil. But it is not the case that any given person, or God himself, cannot meaningfully choose to do good unless he sometimes chooses to do, and does, evil. It is rather that he cannot meaningfully choose good unless he knows what it would be like to do evil, a necessary condition of which is that he should actually have suffered evil at the hands of someone else. (It is conceivable that there should have been in the world only a few people who actually commit evil, provided that their evil activities are widespread.) There is a natural and proper reluctance to say of God that if he is to do good he must sometimes do evil. There should be less resistance to allowing that God if he is to do good must sometimes suffer evil. Indeed, traditional belief combines a denial that Jesus (as Son of God) ever succumbed to the temptation to commit sin with the strong assertion that he did suffer real pain and real rejection at the hands of men. It is necessary, for there to be a meaningful choice of good, that there should be an actualisation of evil actions; but this means that some men must commit evil, not that every man must. No doubt we can take it as empirically certain that all men do. But we are considering an argument that claims that none need do, and the answer to this is that some must.

It might be said against the free will defence that it can offer an answer to part only of the whole problem of evil, namely that part of it that involves so-called moral evil, and that it has no relevance to the problem of natural evil. (Moral evil is the suffering caused by men to each other; natural evil, or physical evil, is the suffering caused to men not by other men but by natural events over which men have no control, such as earthquakes.) In fact, the area covered by the free will defence might be said to be even narrower than this. It seems to cover only part of the problem of moral evil. There is much suffering caused to persons by the actions of others that is not intended. The free will defence talks of men's sometimes choosing evil if they are to be able meaningfully to choose good. But there are often consequences of men's actions which the agents have neither chosen nor foreseen, yet which would never have come about if they had not performed certain actions in the first place. Those consequences, indeed, might have come about whether the original action was chosen or merely happened (i.e. whether it was, properly called, an action at all or merely a piece of behaviour). Such suffering does not easily fit under the heading of natural evil, for it is caused by men. Yet it is hard to see how it can be explained as the effect of men's having chosen to do evil; for they may not have chosen at all, or if they have chosen may have chosen to do good. The suffering caused by men's deliberate choice to inflict evil on their fellow men may be much less than it is sometimes believed to be. Men often perform actions that result in suffering but are at the time believed by them sincerely to be right. The evil that results from either our actions or our behaviour is often then unintended by us—the result of ignorance, well-intentioned stupidity, misplaced enthusiasm, too close an adherence to doubtful principles, etc. But in none of these cases can we be simply said to have chosen evil, knowing it to be evil, in a straightforward confrontation between good and evil. The problem is one of how it comes about that men are able to cause each other suffering, rather than of how it comes about that men choose to do evil. The free will defence commonly puts emphasis upon *choosing* evil rather than good, but the number of cases directly covered by this description may be fewer than is sometimes supposed.

So, even if we accept the free will defence, much of the problem (even of moral evil) would seem to remain unanswered. But there are two lines that can be taken by someone who wants to argue that this is not a serious shortcoming. Some would claim that the free will defence has not in any case generally been offered as a solution to the problem of natural evil, and that it is unreasonable to complain that it fails to solve aspects of a general problem that it has not set out to solve. But (contrariwise) it might be pointed out that it *has* sometimes been claimed that the free will defence can be extended to the problem of natural evil. Thus, Professor Plantinga points out that traditional religious belief has included belief in Satan. 'Unlike most of his colleagues, Satan rebelled against God and has since been creating whatever havoc he could; the result, of course, is physical evil. But now we see that the moves available to the Free Will Defender in the case of moral evil are equally available to him in the case of physical evil' (Plantinga, p. 150, or Mitchell [3], pp. 118–19). And Professor Penelhum similarly reminds us that one element in the free will defence is 'the claim that in order for free moral agents like ourselves to have a real choice of developing the character traits that are stressed in the Christian tradition, there have to be some actual evils for us to react to' (Penelhum, p. 237); and these actual evils will certainly include some natural evils: the free will defence can thus be read as offering a justification of the exis- tence of some natural evils as well as of moral evil.

The present treatment has been brief, but enough may have been said to indicate both why the problem of evil has commonly been considered the most serious of all obstacles to theistic belief, and also something of what might be said by a defender of theistic belief. (For further discussion, see Pike; Plantinga, Chapters 5–6; Hick [2]. For a classical treatment of the problem of evil see Leibniz.)

5. *Wishful thinking*

Next in importance to the problem of evil as an obstacle to theistic belief in my opinion stands the view, or views, of religion associated with the name of Freud: that religion is a kind of neurosis (the universal obsessional neurosis of mankind), a turning of one's back upon reality, a projection upon the universe of childhood parental authoritarianism, a believing of what one wants to believe rather than of what the evidence warrants (see Freud). We may take the last-mentioned idea as the central one for the present discussion. The persuasiveness of Freud's view of religion—he was thinking of Christianity and Judaism—is considerable: there is plausibility in the notion that religious people believe what they want to believe. Of course, it does not follow from the fact that people believe something because (unconsciously) they want to believe it that what they believe is false; and Freud makes no such claim. He does not say that there is no God, but rather that what leads people to believe that there is a God may be something other than they suppose. But although Freud did not claim that if people 'really' believe in God because (unconsciously) they would like it to be the case that there is a God it follows that 'There is a God' is false, his position nevertheless poses problems for the theist.

The notion of a reason for a belief has several senses. We may distinguish (following on remarks made earlier) between a reason for belief in the sense of a logically justifying account and a reason for belief in the sense of a psychological account; and under the latter heading we may distinguish between a man's reason in the sense of *his* reason for holding the belief in question and a man's reason in the sense of *the* reason for his holding the belief in question—that is to say, between the reason the man himself might give and the reason that would be given by an onlooker with knowledge of people's 'real' motivations. The kind of reasons for belief in God that might qualify as logically justifying accounts might be, for example, the traditional theistic proofs. (I mean that the traditional theistic proofs of natural theology are the sort of thing that might be regarded by some as so qualifying: I have already said that I do not myself regard them as logically valid as proofs of God's existence.) If a man were to attempt to justify his belief in God by saying 'The theistic proofs are valid' he would be giving *his* reason for belief in God. But a Freudian might say that *the* reason for his believing in God—the 'real' reason—was quite other than this (infantile seeking for comfort, etc.). A logically justifying account might be quite different from the reasons people themselves give for holding a particular belief and certainly different from the reasons that might be given by a psychologist or sociologist, etc., as those people's real reasons.

There is sometimes (though not always) conflict between different reasons of the same kind. Thus, on some questions there are rival schools of thought, each of which puts forward what are intended as logically justifying accounts, where acceptance of one of these means the rejection of others. But what concerns us at present is the possibility of incompatibility arising on the level of the reasons a man would himself give for holding the beliefs he holds. Frequently, and perhaps usually, where a person gives several different reasons as his reasons for holding a certain belief none of them will be in serious competition with the others: they are, after all, *his* reasons, and we would not expect him to think in widely different, let alone contradictory, ways about a single topic. Nevertheless, people sometimes do. It is possible for a man sometimes to adhere to reasons for a belief which in some respects contradict each other. If a man chooses to give reasons for his religious beliefs there is in one sense nothing to stop him giving bad ones or mutually incompatible ones. But we should nevertheless not think well of someone who chose to give reasons for some important belief and then gave weak or mutually incompatible ones; and we might (however unreasonably) be led by this also to think badly of the belief itself. On the other hand, the giving in public of bad reasons for an important belief can sometimes have the good effect of encouraging the offering of better reasons. Further, when to the onlooker something appears as a bad reason that seems a good one to the believer himself it may not always be right to accept the onlooker's judgement; perhaps the onlooker, by being an 'outsider', is hindered from fully appreciating the reasons for a belief; we return to this question in the final chapter.

Our concern is with a Freudian explanation of religious belief, where this has been converted into one of the reasons that would be given by a believer himself for his belief. It is clear that there is no problem as long as the theist supposes that he believes in God because, for example, he is convinced by the theistic proofs, while being unaware that his 'real' reason is the wish to believe in God. The former reason is his conscious reason, and the latter, being an *un*conscious reason, is, naturally, not present in his mind together with it. But suppose the theist reads Freud, and begins to reflect upon his own religious beliefs in the light of this reading, and is led to acknowledge that there is at least some element of 'wishful thinking' in them. Although no problem arises from saying that a belief which (*unknown to the holder himself*) someone 'really' holds because he wants to hold it, is believed by him to be well-evidenced or well-supported by arguments, there is, I think, an oddness in saying that someone's *conscious* reasons for believing in God are simultaneously that he wants to believe in God (that it would be nice if there were a God) and that the theistic proofs are valid (or that there are other reasons of an orthodox kind). The more Freud's views about the 'real' reasons why people believe in God may come to be acknowledged by a theist as indeed to some extent his own real reasons, the less room there ought to be in that theist's mind for any of the more orthodox reasons. Freud's account of the real reasons for belief is not something of which a little can be added to taste while the previously accepted ingredients remain unaltered. To acknowledge Freud's reasons as one's own would be to reduce the credibility of orthodox theistic reasons which one might wish simultaneously to put forward as also one's own; and this can be expressed by saying that there is a kind of incompatibility in holding Freudian and orthodox reasons together as one's *own* reasons for belief.

The difficulty I have mentioned cannot, of course, arise for the theist if he confines himself to saying that other people's reasons (whether conscious or unconscious) for religious belief may be as Freud says, but that his own (conscious) reasons do not include Freudian reasons.

A common counter to Freud's position consists in pointing out—perfectly correctly as far as it goes—that Freud's is a view about the origins of religious belief, and that the value of something is not exhausted in the value of its origins. Things develop beyond their causes, or their beginnings. To suppose that they do not is to commit what has been called 'the genetic fallacy'. (Harry Truman, when he had achieved the heights of the presidency of the United States, was referred to by some of his detractors as 'a failed haberdasher from Missouri'.) Related to this is the mistake involved in a denial of the principle of organic wholes—that a whole may be greater than the sum of its parts. The value of a work of art, say a great painting, is not to be arrived at by adding together the value of its physical components—so much canvas, so much paint, so much wear and tear on the brushes, so much time spent by the artist at such-and-such a nominal figure per hour. Neither the financial nor the aesthetic value of the painting can be determined by such a method: the completed work is something over and above a collection of parts, and it is the value of this new thing—the artistic whole—that is to be assessed. The assessment requires reference to aesthetic fashion, the state of the market in Old Masters, etc.

But the relevance of the genetic fallacy or the principle of organic wholes needs to be argued for in particular cases. It is not wrong in all cases to maintain that the value of a thing is exhausted by the value of its origins, or that an alleged whole is in reality no more than a collection of parts. In art criticism such things might properly be said in denigration of some piece, and the artist could not retort that the critic was committing a logical error. Each case needs to be considered on its merits. Not all artists, or politicians, develop beyond their beginnings; neither do all religions. There may be an appearance of development, but to point out that it is no more than an appearance may be in a particular case, far from an error, an important and profound judgement. Or it may be maintained that although the development is real and not merely apparent, an account of whatever it is that is under discussion, if it is to be complete, must not lose sight of a more primitive centre beneath the surface. Consider the illumination of religion provided by Otto. Freud's attitude to religion was a hostile one and Otto's was the reverse. But this difference would not justify the acceptance by theists of Otto's work as providing a valuable insight into the primitive heart of all religion and their dismissal of Freud's as a simple committing of the genetic fallacy. If Freud were right in his account of the origins of religious belief he would have provided not a refutation of religion but certainly a reason for taking religion less seriously. What the religious believer maintains might still be true; he might, however, be expected to maintain it with less confidence if he accepted Freud's account; and the outsider would surely be very much less disposed to accept what the religious believer maintains if he (the outsider) also accepted Freud's account.

Nevertheless, to write now critically of him, what Freud had to say does have the defect of concentrating on particular types of religious believer—the mother-fixated, the soft seeker for comfort, the inadequate, the fantast—to the exclusion of other types—the self-disciplined ascetic, the unimaginative conventional moralist, the calm, kindly, Christian hero like Edward Wilson of the Antarctic. His account is plausible as a description of some religious persons, but less so as a description of others. This is not a fatal shortcoming of Freud's doctrine. People are alike in many ways and different in many ways, and a phenomenon as widespread as religious belief is probably not to be expected to be accountable for in one way only. An account that set out to be plausible for *all* the various types of personality to be found among religious people would be a complex one and therefore unlikely to be as striking or as effective as Freud's (or, for that matter, as Marx's 'the opium of the people'). Freud's account is certainly one-sided; but it is also illuminating, at any rate of certain corners. Religious belief does have the function, and is often recommended by religious teachers as having it, of bringing comfort in distress through its apparatus of heaven, heavenly Father, and the like. It is not implausible to suggest that some process is at work whereby what people would like to be the case they come to believe is the case. Compare Freud's story of the poor girl who comes to believe that one day a prince will come and fetch her home (Freud, p. 54). We may be convinced that an unpleasant person will come to a bad end for no better reason than that we should like it to be so. A dying man may convince himself that he is getting better.

Freud's account, because what he offers as the real cause of religious belief is an unconscious motive, is more subtle than an account that would see the matter in terms of a conscious effort in a man to believe that which he wants to believe. We have earlier referred to the question whether belief is a matter of the will (see Chapter 2, section 1), and need not consider this question again. Most religious believers would strenuously deny the suggestion that they are consciously making themselves believe in God; but they are naturally less able to deny the suggestion that they 'really' (but *deep down*, and *unknown* to themselves) believe because they want to believe. (Though it is here that some would say the weakness of Freud's position lies, because of the impossibility of empirical falsification.)

It is an empirical question how far Freud's religious people are typical. It may well be less true now that they are typical than it was previously, and if this is so Freud's own work will have been partly responsible for this change. I have referred to theists becoming aware of Freud's views and, prompted by them, recognising in themselves certain motivations towards, or reasons for, religious belief that they were not previously aware they had. But this can work both ways; and Freud's suggestions can also have, and I suspect may have had, the effect of producing a determination in some that as far as it lies within their power nothing in *their* lives should provide support for views about religion of a Freudian kind. The orthodox Freudian, however, might well reply to this that the efforts of such theists are bound to be in vain: conscious effort will not make the theist aware of, nor can it dampen down the workings of, his own *real* unconscious motives—for this, what is needed is that he should undergo a process of analysis.

5

SOME RELIGIOUS CONCEPTS

1. *Miracle*

In thepreseent chapter I make some comments on some central concepts of religious belief, beginning with miracle.

In some cases several widely different explanations of the same event can be given which do not exclude each other. Thus a man's death may be explained in terms of his having taken poison or in terms of his depression after the death of his wife. There is no need to choose between these, as if they were mutually exclusive alternatives. Both may stand. Which we offer depends on the sort of explanation we want. Now suppose that a man's recovery from illness can be attributed to a certain medical treatment or to a divine miracle. In this case, can we say that there is no necessity to choose between these explanations, that they do not exclude each other? Some, of course, would say that explanation in terms of miracle and explanation in natural terms are mutually exclusive alternatives. Which view we take on this matter depends on the answers to the following questions: how is 'miracle' to be defined? and (closely related) what kind of explanation is explanation in terms of miracle? Let us take the first of these questions.

On a strong definition of 'miracle'—where 'miracle' is defined in some such way as 'an event in which the laws of nature are broken or suspended'—explanation of an event in terms of miracle and explanation of it in natural terms would be mutually exclusive. An event might be explained in terms of the operation of some natural law or in terms of divine suspension of the operation of natural laws: obviously, however, it cannot be explained in both of these ways at the same time; for one of them excludes the other. On a weak definition of 'miracle', however—that is, where 'miracle' is defined in some such way as 'unusual or unexpected event which is seen as having religious significance'—the two explanations are not mutually exclusive: there is no necessary impropriety in saying of a given event both that it can be explained in natural terms and that it is nevertheless at the same time both unusual and of religious significance.

The strong definition of 'miracle' has been questioned on the ground that it involves a notion which is probably nonsensical, that of the divine suspension or breaking of laws of nature—as if laws of nature were prescriptive laws, like the laws of the land, of which it would make sense to say they could be conformed to, or broken, or suspended, or rescinded, rather than, on one important level at any rate, descriptive laws, or generalisations about how nature does in fact behave. The weak definition may seem objectionable on the rather different ground that it *is* weak; it may seem doubtful whether there would be much point for religion in continuing to use the notion of miracle if it meant no more than this. But there would be no virtue in clinging to a strong view if it is a nonsensical one. And the weak view is not as weak as all that. If it limited itself to defining 'miracle' merely as 'unusual or unexpected event' it would no doubt have to be described as barely religiously adequate; but it adds 'of religious significance', and this makes a considerable difference: we shall return to this point later.

Some compromise between the strong and the weak definitions would seem to be desirable, if it can be found. There would be an advantage in trying to retain something from the strong view. The notion of inexplicability seems to be part of what people generally intend by 'miracle', and the notion of inexplicability in natural terms is present in the strong view as it is not in the weak. A compromise might lie in the direction of regarding a miracle as an unusual or unexpected and (in a sense) inexplicable event which has religious significance. Closer attention to the notion of the inexplicable is now needed, and this brings us to the second of the two questions noted above: what kind of explanation is explanation in terms of miracle?

The view I wish to maintain is that a miracle is an event which both is and is not capable of being explained in natural terms. We may take it that every natural event is capable of a natural explanation. That is not to say that the natural explanation must be well known or or even known at all. There may be a large element of uncertainty about it. But if the correct natural explanation has not yet been agreed upon or not yet even discovered, the proper assumption is not that there is no natural explanation but that its establishment lies in the future. We are not, generally, in the discussion of miracles, speculating about some imaginary event, which we can construct in any form we like, even incorporating elements of blatant physical or logical impossibility. We are usually discussing events which are alleged to have actually taken place. They have happened, or are believed to have happened, and what has happened cannot be physically or logically impossible. Also, what has happened could presumably happen again. If something is not impossible and is repeatable, then some natural explanation is presumably capable of being given. The miracles reported in the Bible have all been 'explained away' in various ways (though, of course, such explainings away are a matter of controversy): for example, the feeding of the five thousand has been said to have been achieved by Jesus' setting an example of sharing, or the casting out of devils has been accounted for in terms of hypnotic suggestion. The sense in which alleged miracles might be said to be inexplicable is clearly not such that it would rule out altogether all explanations in natural terms, for such explanations exist. It is rather that natural explanations alone seem inadequate. The force of the stories of Jesus' miracles is such that a purely natural explanation seems to miss the point—the point, that is, of *calling* them miracles.

The sense in which an alleged miracle may be said to be 'inexplicable' is that although it is not literally without the possibility of an explanation, in natural terms such an explanation is not adequate by itself. We may remind ourselves of the difference mentioned earlier between two explanations that might be offered of a man's death. There may be no difficulty in establishing the cause of death as poison, self-administered. But we may still want to say: 'It's inexplicable; he seemed so happy, successful, healthy'. What we are looking for is something that will give us his *reason* for taking his life. Without an acceptable explanation in these terms we may continue to regard the death as 'inexplicable'. If this parallel is apt, then miracles may be regarded as events which although capable of explanation in natural terms seem to call for explanation as well in terms of something like reasons: a man may suppose he glimpses a special divine purpose in them. Sometimes God seems to be seen as operating like a natural cause, though in opposition to, or by 'suspension' of, what our knowledge of natural laws would lead us to expect. On such a view, the paradigm of a miracle would be something like the parting of the waters of the Red Sea, recorded in *Exodus*, taking this for present purposes to be purely an event in which natural laws are supposed to be violated. The waters of a sea do not normally part in order to provide a dry road for a body of people to cross; but God, acting like a kind of divine Superman, using physical or superphysical effort, forces the waters back to lay bare a passage across the sea. This is to regard explanation in terms of miracle as parallel to explanation in terms of natural laws; for the 'suspension' or 'breaking' of natural laws is in order that a physical event may take place through the exercise of super-physical power. But if explanation in terms of miracle is seen as parallel to explanation in terms of reasons we are led to a different point of view. Here the escape of the Israelites against the odds is seen as miraculous, but the stress is not on extraordinary physical events but on a special divine purpose or plan. The parting of the waters alone is not the miracle; this is the means (if we believe the story) to the miracle, which lies in successful escape, because God had a *reason* for the escape of the Israelites, their escape was part of a divine plan, etc.

The choice between miraculous and non-miraculous explanation is sometimes seen as something to be decided on the basis of evidence. A rational man may be expected to choose the likelier of two explanations. The evidence here is presumably evidence of relative frequency of occurrence and conformity or otherwise with natural laws; so the miraculous explanation is pretty well bound to be rejected. If we were to make the assumption that explanation in physical terms and explanation in 'super-physical' terms are parallel, the comparison of evidence would be a fairly straightforward matter. It is not so straightforward, however, if the parallel adopted is one between explanation in terms of miracle and explanation in terms of reasons. Although evidence is relevant to establishing the likelihood of a suggested explanation in terms of reasons, it would not, I think, be natural to speak of deciding between an explanation in terms of causes and an explanation in terms of reasons by a simple method of weighing up evidence. The kind of evidence in the two cases is different; and normally neither bears upon the other. The most usual kind of situation is one where each of the two kinds of explanation is evidenced in a different way, and an investigation of the evidence in the one case does not bear upon the investigation of the evidence in the other. The two kinds of explanation, as we noted, are not mutually exclusive; and the evidence for them similarly is not mutually exclusive. It is only in situations where we are dealing with alternative explanations of the same kind—say, several possible causal explanations—that as explanation A becomes more likely, so explanation B may tend to become less likely. If the cause of death of a body taken from the water was either poison or drowning, and strong evidence comes to hand that points to poison, then, in appropriate circumstances, we might reasonably judge it to be less likely that the cause of death was drowning. Similarly, if the reason for a man's suicide could have been either a belief that he faced financial ruin or a belief that his wife was unfaithful to him, then evidence, from his letters or diaries, that he did indeed believe he faced financial ruin would, in most cases, tend to make it less likely that his reason was a belief that his wife was unfaithful. (Of course, several causes or reasons can operate together, and sometimes in seeking an explanation we are able neither to establish firmly nor to eliminate entirely a certain possibility but can only judge that it is relatively strong or relatively weak.) But, normally, evidence that pointed to poison as the cause of death would not of itself make it either more or less likely that the reason for the man's suicide was belief in impending financial ruin rather than belief in his wife's unfaithfulness. The question of the cause of death and the question of the reason for suicide are different questions: there may be various possible answers·to each, but normally any answer to one is not relevant to finding an answer to the other. Deciding on the best answer to either kind of question separately is a matter of weighing up evidence, but if the parallel between explanation in terms of miracle and explanation in terms of reasons is accepted then deciding between a given explanation of an event in natural terms and an explanation of it in terms of miracle is not done by a simple process of weighing up evidence.

But there is more to be said about the matter than this. Although I have suggested a possible parallel between explanation in terms of miracle and explanation in terms of reasons, we need to note that the parallel does not hold completely. We may decide between various explanations in terms of reasons on the basis of evidence: this is because there may be more than one reason why people do things. But it seems odd to say that there could be several possible explanations of an event in terms of miracle. Explanation in terms of divine miracle is *an* explanation rather than a kind of explanation. We may ask what reason a man had for his actions. We are less likely to ask what purpose God had. We may say that there is *a* divine purpose in some event, but we are unlikely to want to speculate about *which* divine purpose. We are not provided with a list of possible divine purposes (like a list of possible reasons for suicide). Just 'divine purpose' is enough. But if it is the case that there is no clear, agreed list of divine purposes among which we may choose, we do not need the notion of evidence on the basis of which we might choose one divine purpose as more likely than another. To say of an event that it is a natural event is not to explain it so much as to classify it. Explanation is still to follow. But to say of an event that it is a miracle seems to be intended to do more than classify it; it is intended somehow to provide an 'explanation'.

The foregoing may suggest that evidence is not strictly relevant to miracles at all. We do not recognise something as a miracle by carefully examining it and weighing up evidence. It is not as a result of examining evidence that we assign a given event to the category of miracle. How, then, do we do it?

The concept of miracle is a religious concept. The non-religious man is much less likely than the religious man to want to use the term. 'Miracle' is part of the whole apparatus of religious terms: and part of what it means to be a religious man is that such a person is disposed to see the hand of providence at work in the world, and part of what *this* means is that he may be inclined to see some events as miracles. Not all religious believers will make much use of the notion of miracle: the tougher-minded among them may use it hardly at all. But even if not all religious believers make much use of it, it is still a notion that belongs naturally in a religious context, and hardly belongs at all outside it. There is, of course, a use of 'miracle' in non-religious contexts (marvels, 'the miracles of modern science', etc.); but the use of 'miracle' that we are considering here is its use in the context of religious belief.

Hume pointed out to the Christian believers of his day that they do not give credence to stories of miracles told in pagan or super-stitious societies, ancient or modern. Why not? A reason he did not give is that the miracle stories that Christians are inclined to accept are those that support their own religious beliefs. If they are disposed to reject a particular set of non-Christian beliefs, or beliefs that although Christian seem to them superstitious, they will not give credence to the miracle stories associated with those beliefs. Miracles are not to be considered except in relation to a particular religious (cultural, social) background. It has frequently been said that miracles ought not to be appealed to as proofs of Christian belief; the con-nection is rather the other way round: someone who is already a Christian believer will be disposed to take seriously Christian accounts of miracles. (The connection may in fact be a reciprocal one.) As Flew has reminded us, Hume's argument against miracles was not so much that there are no miracles as that 'a miracle can never be proved so as to be the foundation of a system of religion' (Flew, Chapter VIII).

Even if belief in miracles were a straightforward matter of weighing up evidence—and we have expressed doubts on this—it is unlikely to be a matter of weighing up 'objective' evidence, equally available to all. What might seem evidence to one man will not appear as such to another. If a man is disposed to reject a particular set of beliefs as pagan superstition he will not accept as evidence for those beliefs any accounts of miracles: if the beliefs are untrue how can alleged miracles be evidence for their truth? Better to reject the stories of miracles as themselves untrue. The cultural or religious dependence of belief in specific miracles might be offered as an argument against their truth, but only on the assumption that no miracle could possibly be genuine unless it be capable of being seen and acknowledged to be genuine by everybody. But this assumption seems to be the same as the general assumption, which we have in the previous chapter questioned, that nothing could be evidence for the existence of God that would not be acknowledged as evidence by a non-believer as well as a believer. But an important difference between believers and non-believers is that they see the world in different ways. If the non-believer saw as evidence for God—albeit in his opinion insufficient evidence—the same things as the believer sees, then one fundamental difference between the believer and the non-believer would be on the way to disappearing.

The account of miracle that I have been using is one according to which a miracle is an unexpected or unusual and 'inexplicable' event, which is seen as having religious significance. To the non-religious person, by definition, things do not have religious significance, or at any rate certainly not of the kind or to the degree that they have for the religious person. The non-believer can admit the possibility of something like miracles in the limited sense of unexpected or unusual events (though these might better be called marvels), but not in the religious sense of 'inexplicable' unexpected or unusual events having religious significance (except, of course, that he can say of the believer that the latter believes in miracles in that sense).

In brief. The question of the truth or falsehood of a given story of an alleged miracle is not to be settled by an examination of 'objective evidence'. The question of what is to count as evidence is not to be divorced from a consideration of the contents and attitudes of a particular religion: and, furthermore, to the extent that we may regard this as a matter of evidence at all, the acceptability or otherwise of an alleged miracle is not to be discovered simply by a direct comparison between the evidence for a causal account (or account in natural or scientific terms) and the evidence, in the shape, say, of testimony, for an explanation in terms of miracle; for this is probably to regard explanation in terms of miracle as itself a kind of explanation in causal terms, that is, in terms of the super-physical effort of a super-physical being, which is an inadequate view of what explanation in terms of miracle is. It may well be that religious believers need not insist with any great force upon the truth of many, if any, alleged Christian miracles. But it has not been my concern to discuss this. I have not been arguing for the truth, or for that matter for the falsehood, of any particular miracle stories. I have tried rather to confine myself to the question of what sort of belief belief in miracles is.

G

2. *The soul and immortality*

The importance of the concept of the soul for religious belief to a considerable extent arises from its connection with the notions of immortality and divine grace. We shall have something to say about grace later in the chapter. Immortality we shall consider now. (On immortality see Geach; also Flew and MacIntyre, pp. 261–72.)

Although belief in immortality is less orthodox in Christianity than is belief in the resurrection of the body, it is fairly often to be found, in combination with a dualist view of the human person (the view that a person is body *plus* soul): immortality has to be immortality of the soul, for whatever else the body may be it is patently not immortal. But if there is to be any sense in talk of the immortality of an individual human person, it would seem that that person's soul must be regarded as not just an equal partner with his body in his total constitution (for in that case the immortality of that person would only be the immortality of half of him) but as constituting on its own the *real* person. Thus the usual kind of belief in immortality is belief that human beings 'really' consist of souls, which are embodied but which can exist disembodied, and indeed must be able to.

There are difficulties about the notion of a disembodied *person* (we may now safely say disembodied 'person' rather than disembodied 'soul', as the view we are considering involves the identification of the soul with the real person). A disembodied person would lack the senses, and without the senses it could not experience or communicate. The difficulty is not that disembodied souls could not exist; it is one of meaningfully identifying a disembodied soul with a human person. The kind of attenuated existence a disembodied soul would be limited to is not the kind of existence that human persons have—an existence of acting and suffering (climbing mountains, writing or reading poetry, fighting, playing games, watching other people play games, talking to each other, etc.). But even if we were to accept as properly human the kind of existence a disembodied soul would have, there is then the problem of how a disembodied soul could be identified with a *particular* human person. Even if we were to be persuaded that disembodied souls qualify for the description 'human person'—perhaps as a kind of sub-class of human beings, as, under different sorts of categorial arrangement, men and women, or black and white, or active and lazy might be said to be sub-classes of human beings—how are we to be persuaded that a given disembodied soul is identical with a given named particular human being? This identification is necessary if the existence of disembodied souls is to be relevant to the question of individual human immortality. If souls exist it may be allowed that they are immortal; for, as 'soul' has commonly been used, the notion of indestructibility is written into its meaning. If the term 'soul' is to be used at all, we may allow that problems about the immortality of the soul are not serious ones; but there are problems about the immortality of the person.

A list of the contents of the universe might be said to include souls. But when religious believers talk of the immortality of the soul they generally do not have in mind merely the existence of souls as items in the universe. They are thinking of the immortality of particular named human individuals. The difficulties, then, arise over the identification of particular named human individuals with (their) souls. As we have noted already, unless the soul is the real person, the survival of his bodily death by a person's soul is at best only the survival of half of him. This may be in fact to put it rather generously. It might be fairer to say—except that one can hardly quantify in this way—that what might survive would be only a quarter, or an eighth, or maybe even a hundredth of a human person. The formula 'body *plus* soul' does not have to be taken as meaning body and soul in equal proportions. Saints, perhaps, are more soul than body.

The orthodox Christian view is one in which the enjoyment of the delights of heaven is presented as conditional. We have to make ourselves (with God's help: see, on this, later sections) worthy of closer proximity to God. The process of becoming worthy is one of becoming a new man. It is in part one of purging ourselves of wrongful desires, etc. Boswell quotes from Johnson's *Meditations*:

My indolence, since my last reception of the sacrament, has sunk into grosser sluggishness, and my dissipation spread into wilder negligence. My thoughts have been clouded with sensuality: and, except that from the beginning of this year I have in some measure forborne excess of strong drink, my appetites have predominated over my reason. A kind of strange oblivion has overspread me, so that I know not what has become of the last year; and perceive that incidents and intelligence pass over me without leaving any impression.

Boswell goes on: 'He then solemnly says, "This is not the life to which heaven is promised" . . .; and he earnestly resolves an amendment.' Johnson—that pious but worldly man—was seeking to cultivate self-discipline, not withdrawal from the world; he disliked people who withdrew to convents and monasteries. Cultivation of the soul in the view of some may require withdrawal from the world; in the view of others, like Johnson, it requires nothing of the kind.

There is no need to interpret talk of the cultivation of one's soul as talk about the cultivation of a *part* of oneself. It is rather cultivation of some aspects of life—or cultivation of certain propensities and interests rather than others. Work on the philosophy of mind by Wittgenstein, Ryle and others has shown up the misleading character of over-simple dualist talk. But an abandonment of the view of the soul (or the mind) as a kind of thing, linked with something else, the body (in Ryle's phrase, a 'ghost in the machine'), does not mean the abandonment of talk about souls. To describe people as having, or as being, souls is to call attention to certain aspects of them rather than others. Thus, to speak of the population of an area as consisting of 'some three thousand souls' is to indicate a certain attitude towards those three thousand people, or perhaps towards people in general. It seems to suggest that the speaker thinks the spiritual welfare of his fellow men is more important than their material welfare. This use of the term 'soul' implies a view of persons according to which achieving eternal salvation, or missing it, is the central thing of human concern. (Compare: 'poor lost soul'; not 'poor lost body' or 'poor lost person'.)

A rehabilitation of the view of the soul as a literal, separable *part* of the whole person is as impossible (since Ryle) as it is unnecessary (cf. Lucas, in Mitchell [1], pp. 132–48).

The cultivation of the soul is a matter of avoidance of sin and preparation for the entry of divine grace—according to Christian doctrine. The notions of sin and grace are quasi-moral in character, but will not be found in books on moral philosophy. They are concepts rather of moral theology. The same is true even of the related notion of virtue, which is nowadays largely ignored by moral philosophers but still discussed by moral theologians ('Christian virtues'). In the remainder of this chapter I discuss the religious concepts of sin, grace and (chiefly) virtue.

3. *Humility; sin*

The expression 'Christian virtues' is not always used to cover precisely the same set of things. There is no single Biblical source for a list of the Christian virtues. I do not propose to embark on my own account on an attempt to provide a definitive list. This has in any case been sufficiently established by the moral theologians; for the generally agreed view among them seems to be that the Christian virtues are seven in number—three theological virtues, faith, hope and love, together with the four cardinal virtues, prudence, fortitude, temperance and justice. Any list of Christian virtues is likely to contain items that one would not find on a list of Greek virtues: some virtues, that is, seem to be peculiarly Christian virtues in the sense that only Christians recognise them as virtues, or at least lay stress on them. For instance, Aquinas in the *Summa Theologica* classes as virtues, parts of virtues, or acts of virtue, the following, among others: faith, hope, religion, vengeance, martyrdom, fasting, virginity, humility. Not all of these would be so classed by non-

Christians; for that matter, not all of them might be so classed by all Christians. The most interesting item here is, I think, humility.

Humility depends upon circumstances. What would be humble behaviour coming from one man might, coming from another, be considered to border on the arrogant. The virtue of the humble act depends indeed, to borrow Aristotle's language, on its being done at the right time, with reference to the right objects, towards the right people, with the right motive, and in the right way. The Christian stress on humility is clearly a reflection of the general Christian emphasis on inwardness, and on human imperfection and lack of self-sufficiency: what counts is not how you stand among men but how you stand with God; and a man is not likely to glory in his own attainments if he is impressed by the thought of human dependence on God.

But the concept of humility is a difficult one to get clear. It is treated differently by different writers. It is obviously an important Christian virtue—one much insisted on, for instance, in the writings of Christian mystics. But it does not find a place in the list of seven Christian virtues with which traditional moral theology provides us. It is dismissed by Dr R. C. Mortimer (*The Elements of Moral Theology*) in a few short sentences in the course of his chapter on fortitude. Dr Kenneth Kirk (in *Some Principles of Moral Theology*) refers to it, in a single sentence, in his chapter on faith—and even then he is writing about intellectual humility only. Aquinas himself treats it as a species of modesty, which in its turn he treats as a secondary virtue annexed to temperance. Etienne Gilson has written: 'Just as the superiority he sees in others is from God, the humble man knows that he is great in bowing before others because all virtue is great and particularly humility before God.' The humble man knows that he is great: this is paradoxical. 'Humility' and 'humble' rather often bear a pejorative sense, which is not the case with 'courage' or even 'temperance'. I have heard someone say that humility is a vice.

The question that particularly interests me here is whether Christian humility is as unique as people often assume—and as I have myself been assuming so far. Humility is normally opposed to pride. But humility, as we know, can easily pass into pride (a man can become proud of his humility, and this is presumably one of the forms taken by what is called spiritual pride). Equally there can be a kind of pride—a proper pride as contrasted with undue pride—that may not be at all sharply opposed to humility—that may, indeed, not be opposed to it at all. The truly humble Christian man is the man who has the right kind and the right amount of humility: he is properly described as humble towards God, in the first place, rather than towards men; and in so far as he is humble towards men this does not necessarily mean that he considers himself inferior to them. If he happens to find himself set in authority over other men he will exercise this authority—he will not say that as a humble man he must beg to be excused his duty. The humble man does not evaluate himself in exactly the same way in relation to every other man: this would be inappropriate. Obsequiousness, over-demeaning of oneself, is as little virtuous as is, at the opposite extreme, being puffed up with a sense of one's own importance.

Is there really so immense a difference between the Christian virtue of humility and, say, Aristotle's virtues concerned with honour —proper pride, proper ambitiousness—as is generally supposed? Certainly, if only social relationships are considered, though this is perhaps too large an if, the differences may well seem to diminish. Also, if this kind of humility is *rational* behaviour, as it surely is, the difference may, again, not strike us as so very considerable. Humility in this sense might be represented as part of the universal make-up of human nature (though, admittedly, the Greeks did not think of humility as a virtue). To seek to use one's talents to the full and, in order to achieve this, to assume an appropriate position in society—neither too high nor too low—seems a proper end for a rational being to set before himself. What appears in Christianity under the name of humility is perhaps one version of something that takes different forms at different times and in different places, but that fundamentally reduces to the rational attitude just referred to.

It might be said, by way of objection, that this is true—if true at all—*only* on the level of social relationships. What about the saint and the mystic, to whom God is so much more important than society? But this is not a serious objection. It may not be wholly irrelevant to point out that it was not Christians who first gave the highest place to the contemplative, and presumably largely non-social, life; but, in any case, saints and mystics have always been somewhat exceptional in Christianity, and their kind of life has not, in general, ever had much official recommendation. It is the 'ordinary' Christian, in and of society, who needs to be considered here.

There is another objection, however, and one that is more serious. Nothing has been said so far about 'sin' and 'grace', terms whose relation to 'vice' and 'virtue' is by no means clear but which cannot be ignored in any discussion of Christian virtues. Humility is a Christian virtue, but its opposite—pride—would more naturally be called by Christians not a vice but a sin. (The opposite of 'Christian virtue' is not 'Christian vice'; and it is not 'non-Christian vice' either.) 'Sin' is sometimes used, by some theologians as well as by others, to mean more or less what is meant by 'moral wrongdoing' or some such phrase: but too close an assimilation of these terms to each other is surely a mistake. There is more than one way of defining 'sin', but it seems safe to say that any adequate account of it must bring out the fact that it belongs to the language of religion rather than to that of morals, and also that it has something to do with God and with man's relation to God. Suppose now it is claimed that this shows the Christian virtue of humility to be unique—unique in being contrasted in the Christian's mind not with a vice but with a sin? (This would perhaps be only another way of saying that my earlier qualification 'if only social relationships are considered' is unacceptable, and that unless God is brought into the matter what we are talking about is not really a *Christian* virtue.) It would, of course, be foolish to deny that the Christian sees humility as primarily an attitude towards God, and to this extent Christian humility is bound to be different from anything which may be like it in other respects but does not share this reference. But, on the other hand, all humility—whether Christian or not—involves a reference to *something*. An artist, if he feels humble, does so in relation to other artists whom he judges greater than himself, or he might even say, more mysteriously, that he feels humble in relation to Art itself. God is here perhaps a kind of limiting case. As far as their behaviour is concerned the humble Christian and the humble non-Christian may not be markedly different. At the same time, the fact that the Christian, when he makes a rational assessment of himself, adds 'but I am a sinner', whereas the Greek, in making a rational assessment of himself, did not, does constitute an objection to the view that Christian humility is not unique, and I shall not pretend that it does not.

The notorious difficulty that the Early Church had in assimilating the pagan cardinal virtues has sometimes given rise to doubts about why Christians should have tried to take them over at all. An answer in purely historical terms (the influence of Ciceronian ethics on St Ambrose, of Neo-Platonism on St Augustine, etc.) seems hardly to go deep enough. But if it is the case that the virtues—at any rate the cardinal virtues—represent, or are supposed to represent, fundamental and inescapable features of moral or rational (or human) life, at all times and in all places, then it is not surprising that Christians took them over; it would have been surprising if they had not. (It is significant that it was a Christian who first called the cardinal virtues 'cardinal virtues'.) The theological virtues may be difficult to fit into this picture: moral theologians would certainly claim these as uniquely Christian; and it may well appear that they cannot easily be presented as no more than Christian versions of some universal features of the well-lived human life. Even so, faith (in something or other), hope (in something or other), love (in something like the

Christian sense)—these, it might be urged, must find a place in any
account of the virtuous life, and the fact that Aristotle did not recognise them only reminds us that he was not interested in discovering
universal virtues.

4. *Infusion and grace*

What is peculiarly Christian about Christian virtues, it is often
claimed, is not what I have assumed in the foregoing section,
namely that they constitute a special list of virtues which only
Christians recognise, but rather that they possess a special property
not possessed by non-Christian virtues. This way of putting the
matter is, it may reasonably be said, the more important; for merely
to belong to one list rather than another seems to be less fundamental
than is the possession of some special unique property.

The difference between Christian virtues and non-Christian virtues, as I shall now consider it, hinges on a distinction that is an
essential element in traditional moral theology—that between
acquired and infused virtues. In general, the theological virtues are
infused, the moral virtues are acquired; but this position is complicated by the further view that the moral (cardinal) virtues may,
it is claimed, themselves be infused, and indeed are, in so far as they
are *Christian* virtues. The distinction is usually expressed in some
such way as this: infused virtues are gratuitously implanted in us
by God, whereas acquired virtues are acquired by constant practice.
The marks of an infused virtue are somewhat variously stated, but
the following four differences between infused and acquired virtues
have been suggested: (1) infused virtues are not habits but dispositions; (2) they are directed to a different end; (3) they have a different
motive; (4) they judge according to a different standard. I proceed
now to a discussion of these points. I shall confine myself in the
meantime to the moral virtues.

(1) It has been maintained that infused virtues are not so much
habits as potentialities, faculties, or dispositions. This suggests, on
the surface, that the man with the infused virtue of temperance is
the man of whom the best you can say is that he would be temperate
if the opportunity arose, whereas the man with the acquired virtue
of temperance is the man for whom opportunities do arise and who
actually is temperate. This position has been taken further than this.
Mortimer writes of the difference between infused and acquired
virtues as one of relative difficulty and ease. And this is almost as if
one might say that the man with the infused virtue of temperance is
the man who could not really be relied upon to be temperate even
if opportunities for temperance did occur; for he finds it so hard.

No one is likely to deny that what we do habitually we tend to do easily; and what we do not do habitually we tend not to do so easily. But it is not clear how this throws light on the difference between infused and acquired virtues. Why should a gift of temperance, implanted in us by God without any effort on our part, be more difficult to exercise than temperance acquired by a possibly long and arduous process of habituation? This position suggests that there is merit in mere difficulty, and this does not chime in well with the notion of the infused virtues as *gifts*.

In isolating this first suggested difference between infused and acquired from the other three I am no doubt not being altogether fair. But what I am chiefly anxious to do is to show that the disposition/habit distinction does not point to a clear difference between infused and acquired virtues. The prudent or courageous or temperate or just man could naturally be described either as the man who, among other things, has a disposition to behave in certain ways, or as the man who, among other things, habitually does behave in certain ways; and although there is certainly a difference between these descriptions, each, so far as I can see, could be quite naturally applied to what the moral theologians mean by acquired virtues, and so cannot without strain be said to point to a difference between these and infused virtues. The suggestion about ease and difficulty may, indeed, call attention to a real difference between acquired and infused virtues, but there is not, as seems to be supposed by Mortimer, a necessary connection between being difficult to exercise and being a potentiality, disposition, or faculty.

Aquinas himself does not, as far as I can see, invoke a habit/disposition distinction to explain the difference between infused and acquired virtues. Significantly, Mortimer, when he comes to his chapter on faith—which is, of course, an infused virtue—immediately begins writing of faith as a habit, though he ought on his own principles to be saying that it is not a habit.

(2) The second alleged difference between infused and acquired virtues depends on the principle that causes must be proportionate to their effects. The acquired virtues are fitted to the attainment of ordinary human happiness; but they are not fitted to the attainment of man's ultimate and perfect happiness. No naturally acquired virtues can lead man to a supernatural end; for this, supernaturally induced virtues are needed. This second difference can conveniently be considered together with the third.

(3) Moral theologians maintain that the outward actions of a man with an infused virtue may be indistinguishable from those of a man with the corresponding acquired virtue. But, it is claimed, there will be a difference in their respective motives. As Aquinas says: 'Both

acquired and infused temperance moderate desires for pleasures of touch, but for different reasons.' Mortimer states the difference thus: 'It is that between doing an action because we see that it is good for us or for society, either now or in the long run, and doing it because it is the will of God, and we would not be separated from Him.'

The second and third differences, as I have stated them, can be seen not to be identical, though in fact they are not always distinguished from each other by the moral theologians. There is a difference between ends and motives. An end of human action need not be anything consciously adopted. A motive, on the other hand, is generally consciously and intentionally adopted. (If we leave out of account unconscious motives then we may say that a motive is *always* consciously and intentionally adopted.)

The claim that infused virtues differ from acquired in respect of motive is hard to understand. If infused virtues are gratuitously imparted by God, how can motives come into the matter? It is hard to see what it means to say both that an infused virtue involves that we ourselves adopt one motive rather than another and at the same time that God gratuitously imparts the infused virtue. If it be suggested that conscious adoption, or choice, does not come into it, but God freely imparts the motive, too, then I can only say that I do not know what is meant by a *motive* that is thus implanted in us and is not consciously adopted by us. Such a thing would not be a motive at all, except in a sense analogous to that of 'unconscious motive'. But in any case, unconscious motives are not what the moral theologian has in mind. Doing a thing for the reason that it is commanded by God can hardly be intended to be interpreted as meaning: doing a thing from the unconscious motive that it is commanded by God, though consciously perhaps from some quite different motive.

The claim that the difference lies in the respective *ends* is also far from clear. The notion of ends is parallel to that of unconscious motives, to the extent that no conscious adoption of that end is necessarily implied in saying that a man's life is directed towards a certain end. The difficulty here, however, is one of seeing how a difference in their ends can in practice be successfully appealed to in order to distinguish an infused from an acquired virtue. If it were simply a matter of a conscious, intentional aiming at one end rather than another some difference would doubtless be plain enough; though in that case the claim about ends would probably reduce to the claim about motives. But in a case where ends are not consciously chosen and where even perhaps (what is possible) we have no knowledge that they are drawing us towards them, it is difficult to see how we could say with certainty of a given virtue that it tended

towards one end rather than another. There is nothing we can appeal
to in their outward manifestations; for, as we have already noted,
an infused virtue and an acquired virtue may issue in actions
indistinguishable from each other.

(4) The fourth difference between infused and acquired virtues is
that of standards. There is a mean fixed by human reason, says
Aquinas, which in the case of consumption of food requires that
it should not harm the health of the body nor interfere with the
exercise of reason; and this is the acquired virtue of temperance.
There is also a divine rule whereby man is commanded to chastise his
body and bring it into subjection; and this is the infused virtue of
temperance.

This difference comes very close to the third, the difference in
motives; so close that I doubt whether it really deserves a separate
heading. It is admitted by moral theologians, as we have seen more
than once, that the outward actions of the man with an infused virtue
may be indistinguishable from those of the man with the corresponding acquired virtue. It is now said that the men differ nevertheless
in their standards. Generally speaking, when people are said, in a
moral or quasi-moral context, to have different standards, this is
taken to imply that their outward behaviour is different. There is,
of course, no reason why two men applying different standards should
not arrive at the same behaviour: why their temperance, for instance,
should not show itself in the same ways, even down to quite small
details, even though one of them is behaving as he does because he
is following the mean laid down by human reason, while the other
is behaving as he does because he is following the divine rule to
chastise his body and bring it into subjection. At the same time, the
natural thing to say in such a case would be not that their standards
are different but that there are different reasons for which, or different motives from which, they are behaving—the one for the reason
that he wants to preserve his bodily health and mental efficiency,
and he sees that this is the best way to do it, and the other for the
reason that God has commanded the subjugation of the body.

So far in this discussion of infused *versus* acquired virtues I have
been considering only the cardinal virtues; and the cardinal virtues,
according to moral theologians, may be either acquired or infused.
The theological virtues, on the other hand, are, it is maintained,
always only infused. And this means, I take it, that the mark of a
Christian as opposed to a non-Christian virtue should be seen more
clearly in the theological virtues than in the cardinal virtues.

It is a matter of definition that the theological virtues—faith, hope
and love—are infused and not acquired. But, clearly, there are

acquired virtues that correspond to these three infused virtues. For, outside the religious field (or, for that matter, within it, according to some theological views), there clearly are kinds of faith, hope and love which, acquired in the first place by conscious effort, by constant practice grow easier to exercise. In so far as we may judge faith, hope and love (as directed towards some things rather than others) to be valuable, we may consider that we have a duty to practise them constantly and to acquire facility in their exercise. But the faith, hope and love we may thus think we ought to cultivate cannot be the infused virtues bearing those names. These, by definition, are gifts of God and cannot be acquired by human effort; and there can consequently be no duty to cultivate them. It would seem, indeed, that the notion of 'religious duties', in so far as this may be applied to the three theological virtues, ought to strike the moral theologian as doubtfully meaningful. It ought to. But does it so strike him?

It does not. In fact, religious duties are insisted on; and those duties are certainly held to include duties of faith, hope and love. 'Duties towards God Himself involve the cultivation of the three theological virtues, or in the words of the Catechism, "my duty towards God is to believe in Him, to fear Him and to love Him"' (Mortimer, p. 27). This must surely mean that we have a duty to improve ourselves in the respects mentioned, and that we are capable of effecting such improvement by our own efforts (otherwise we could have no duty in the matter). But what then becomes of the difference between infused and acquired? To speak of the infused virtues as if we can cultivate them is to speak of them as if they were acquired virtues. The distinction between the two disappears.

This criticism fails, of course, if it is held that the infused virtues are divine gifts in some sense which does not preclude their also being cultivable (I shall be returning to this later)—e.g. they may be originally induced by God, but thereafter developed by human effort.

A related form of the present difficulty comes out in the case of faith. Aquinas says that what causes man to assent to 'the things which are of faith' is God: against the Pelagians he holds that we do not have the power to assent of our own free will; we cannot have, 'since man, by assenting to matters of faith, is raised above his nature', and 'this must needs accrue to him from some supernatural principle moving him inwardly; and this is God. Therefore faith, as regards the assent which is the chief act of faith, is from God moving man inwardly by grace' (*Summa Theologica*, II–II, vi, 1). But if God supplies the assent, it is hard to see what can be meant by saying that man assents. It is rather as if God is assenting to his own proposition and the presence of man is incidental. I am not simply calling attention to the implication that there is something God-like in faith (which is what the moral theologians themselves might say); I am calling attention rather to the implication that there can be little that is man-like in it. And if this is so, the question suggests itself: What merit is there in being a mere passive instrument of, or container for, faith? How can faith, in fact, be a virtue? It is often held that there is no special merit in believing something that can be demonstrated as true. The *value* of assent to the things of religious faith would lie, then, in its involving an effort of will to overcome doubt. But it would be odd thus to put a value on acts of religious assent while at the same time insisting that such acts are not within the unaided power of a man, but are, to put it perhaps too strongly, God assenting to God. I am not sure how far this confusion is present in the moral theologians; but Mortimer, I think, comes close to it.

It is only fair to say that not all moral theologians want to insist on the difference between infused and acquired virtues—and hence between Christian and non-Christian virtues—in just the way I have been discussing. But this is certainly the traditional line: Aquinas himself maintained that acquired virtue is not of the same species as infused virtue. It clearly is possible, however, to have a weaker kind of view that does not depend upon the segregation of infused from acquired virtues. The notion of being freely given does not always exclude that of being acquired by human effort. To take a crude analogy: a small child may struggle to tie his shoe-lace for a long time, and then his mother comes along and does it for him. The lace is tied—that is a gift from the child's mother, and one not necessarily given as a reward that the child has earned for his effort; for the mother may tie the lace absent-mindedly. At the same time, the child, by its efforts, however fruitless, is slowly acquiring a skill, a skill that can only be acquired by constant practice. The fact that the parent has made the gift of tying the shoe-lace does not render the child's efforts useless, any more than the child's efforts render the parent's gift unnecessary. When the skill has eventually been acquired we may say of it that it could not have been acquired without both gifts and effort. (Compare also a talent—'gift'—which remains merely potential unless drawn out and developed by years of training.) Such a moral theology would escape some of the criticism I have been making. It would, however, mark a definite change from the line followed traditionally by moral theologians: this sense of 'infused virtue' would not, as far as I can see, be that which the term has traditionally been given.

Another way of interpreting the relationship between infused and acquired virtues would be to understand infused virtues as a kind of bonus superimposed on acquired virtues. That is to say, the Christian achieves a certain point in his Christian development by his own efforts, through the cultivation of acquired virtues, and then these efforts are crowned (by grace) by a reward in the form of infused virtues. This, clearly, conflicts with the view of the traditional moral theologian who wants to say, for instance, that even a newly-baptised infant can receive infused virtues; obviously the infant cannot be receiving these as a bonus for acquired virtues already possessed. But we may feel inclined to say: so much the worse for the traditional moral theologian! And, indeed, this traditional line is very closely associated with a mechanical view of divine grace, that would be repudiated by many theologians. If a mechanical view of grace is abandoned, so is the notion of infused virtues as traditionally understood. However, the traditional view is by no means dead.

There can be no doubt that behind this traditional view there lie good intentions. It is only fair to say that the traditional theory of infusion was probably invented as a way of explaining some central kinds of Christian experience—for instance, the experience of conversion (possibly sudden and violent, and involving a change in the direction of a man's life; and not easily to be accounted for in terms of the laborious and gradual acquiring by one's own efforts of faith); or the experience of having some special supernatural assistance in work undertaken, an experience so intense that the Christian may feel impelled to say, 'Not I, but God (or Christ, or the Holy Spirit) working in and through me' (St Paul often says things of this sort). The traditional theory of infusion begins, we may be reasonably sure, as a way of making sense of all this, and to that extent is an important attempt at reducing to some sort of order striking, and probably new, kinds of experience. But somewhere along the line the matter has got out of hand.

6

RELIGION AND SCIENCE

1. *Scientific attitudes and religious attitudes*

Since the seventeenth century the relation between religion and science
has been of interest to theologians, and, at any rate in the earlier
part of the period, to scientists also. What is sometimes referred to
as the 'warfare' or 'conflict' between science and theology is no
longer being waged; for the most part it existed only as long as
theologians, and to a lesser extent scientists, were unclear about the
possibilities and the limits of their own studies. But if the war had
not been waged they would not have had as much incentive as they
did have to force themselves and each other towards greater clarity.

If we are to understand the nature of religious belief or of claims
to religious knowledge, we need to see them in relation to belief or
knowledge of other kinds, and the beliefs and knowledge of scientists (and the methods of scientists) provide the most relevant contrast. Some of the main questions with which science dealt in the
seventeenth century and later seemed to be questions to which
theology had already offered answers: the nature and origins of the
physical universe, and (later) the origins of living creatures and of
man. There were other questions of theology, notably about man's
destiny as opposed to his origins, which science did not attempt to
answer; but the overlap was important enough, or so it seemed, to
indicate that science could not be ignored by theologians. This
similarity of subject matter seemed of significance to scientists as
well as to theologians, and some scientists supposed themselves to
be engaged in the business of uncovering the workings of the divine
mind in the universe. Scientific laws were God's laws. For instance,
scientists as well as theologians contributed to the development of
the Argument from Design (see Hurlbutt).

There may be (apparent) similarities of subject matter between theology and science—for example, in cosmology. However, the relation between them that I shall discuss is rather that between scientific method and theological method, including that between scientific attitudes and religious attitudes.

On one level both science and religion show themselves as attitudes to the world and to life. A man's being a scientist may condition his approach to many things: he may be sceptical in his general attitudes, unwilling to accept what he is told on any subject until he has sub- jected it to whatever tests he can. 'The scientific attitude' is an attitude that can and may be applied by a scientist to many things other than those that he is concerned with in his professional life as a scientist. But, of course, the sciences are principally professional pursuits with particular subject matters. Further, some scientists rather con- spicuously do not show any particular appreciation of the need for weighing evidence, etc., in matters other than those that they are professionally concerned with. The situation as far as the religious man is concerned may seem to be similar. The religious man may be a man whose attitude to the world and to life is of a certain kind— for whom, to quote Paley again, the world becomes a temple. On the other hand, however, some religious people are people for whom religion is a separate department of their lives: they may carry out religious duties on appropriate occasions but it would rarely occur to them unprompted to adopt a 'religious' attitude towards secular questions. One is inclined to say that whereas it is not a delinquency in a scientist that he should fail to carry 'the scientific attitude' into his everyday life, it is a delinquency in a religious man that he should regard his religious attitude as something to be adopted only on Sundays or only in connection with certain things. *Seriously* to regard the whole world as a temple would seem to rule out the possi- bility of regarding it in this way on only some occasions.

The fact that some people have combined a distinguished career in science with a sincere attachment to religious belief is not enough to demonstrate that there is no incompatibility between the two. As we have remarked earlier, it is not unknown for people to adhere to two different sets of beliefs or to exhibit two different attitudes which are mutually incompatible but which they themselves do not see to be incompatible. It is certainly not uncommon for people to admit one or two small incompatible elements into what is otherwise a consistent set of beliefs or attitudes; the fewness or smallness of these elements is perhaps the reason for their continuing to be tolerated, as if logical errors were like moral ones—at one extreme logical peccadilloes, at the other logical mortal sins. I am not asserting that there is a logical incompatibility between the beliefs or attitudes of religion and the beliefs or attitudes of science. But nevertheless, there might be a kind of psychological incompatibility, or at any rate tension.

To some extent the contrast between the scientific attitude and the religious attitude is one between different temperaments. Some see it as a contrast between the attitude of open inquiry seeking truth and the attitude of unquestioning faith unwilling or unable to face reality. Freud saw the contrast between science and religion in some such terms as these, and was in no doubt as to which was the attitude of a rational man. Freud's own view of science was a somewhat idealised one:

The transformation of scientific ideas is a process of development and progress, not of revolution . . . a rough approximation to the truth is replaced by one more carefully adjusted, which in its turn awaits a further approach to perfection. . . . No, science is no illusion. But it would be an illusion to suppose that we could get anywhere else what it cannot give us (Freud, pp. 96–8).

Writers on the relation between science and religion have frequently wanted to point out that the relation is not a simple one: that there is an element of faith in science or an element of questioning and doubt in religion, etc. But such remarks, though what is said is perfectly true, may have the effect of softening overmuch what is still a real difference. The aim behind such attempts has generally been to achieve a reconciliation between science and religion, but in practice it has been a reconciliation in which religion is accommodated to science rather than the other way about. Religion has been on the defensive in the 'warfare' between science and religion: naturally enough, for theistic religion was there first, and it was not until the seventeenth century that science was able to begin to apply methods of its own. Science appeared as the brash newcomer, challenging accepted orthodoxies of attitude and method. But the great success of science led, as we know, by the nineteenth century, to a situation where religion had very much its back to the wall, and the aim of liberal theological writers was to find in religion attitudinal strands (of experience and the like) that could be represented as according with those of science, just as, as far as actual concrete subject matter is concerned, the aim was to withdraw any claim of religion to put forward views about such matters as the origins of man that might be in conflict with the views apparently accepted by scientists.

No doubt what has here been represented as the scientific attitude existed before the seventeenth century: there have presumably always been men who were by nature questioning, and who wanted to use

H

methods of empirical inquiry, etc. Such men were no doubt able to find some scope for their attitude within institutional frameworks of some other kind. But the considerable development of science has given ever larger numbers of such people an institutional home of a kind they did not possess before; and the development of scientific education has contributed to the cultivation in many people of an attitude of this kind who in previous ages would never have had it cultivated.

The view so far assumed of 'the scientific attitude' is a popularly accepted one, but Professor Liam Hudson has given a very different account of it. He suggests that the schoolboy inclined to scientific subjects is a 'converger', the schoolboy inclined to arts subjects a 'diverger'. The terms 'converger' and 'diverger' are presented initially with reference to psychologists' mental tests: the converger is much better at ordinary intelligence tests than at (certain) open-ended tests or tests of 'creativity'; the diverger is the reverse (Hudson, p. 55). Hudson comments as follows on some autobiographical efforts of his schoolboy subjects.

[Of the converger:] At some stage in his life he seems to have turned his back on the sphere of personal relations, and focused all his attention on areas where people and personal emotions are least likely to obtrude. . . . We note . . . that his reactions to controversial issues are often stereotyped, and that he is prone to compartmentalize one topic from another. Both habits of mind serve, presumably, to minimize the uneasiness which ambiguous or conflicting ideas create; and both may be seen as defences against anxiety. . . . [T]he converger's attitudes tend to be conventional, and authoritarian. . . . He is disconcerted by open-ended tests, not simply because they offer emotional possibilities which he distrusts, but, particularly, it seems, because they offer a task which lacks a single right answer. [Of the diverger:] He moves naturally towards the human aspects of his culture—literature, politics—and shuns the technical and practical. He is liberal in his attitudes; and seems less prone than the converger to accept beliefs on trust, or to think in conventional terms. And, above all, he seems actively to enjoy the expression of his personal feelings; or, at least, to enjoy expressing his feelings about matters which are personal. Where the converger avoids personal discussion, the diverger positively seeks it out. . . . However, the diverger's position has its weaknesses. The chief of these lies in his reaction to precise, logical argument. He is weak at this, and in some cases, seems positively alarmed by it. Where the converger enjoys precision, the diverger views it as a trap. In caricature: the converger takes refuge from people in things; the diverger takes refuge from things in people (Hudson, pp. 102–9).

There is a considerable difference between the popular picture of the scientist as a man engaged in 'pushing back the frontiers of knowledge', always seeking something new—and the associations of the term 'converger', as of someone lacking in imagination, clinging to accepted views, a learner of facts as opposed to a free-ranging intellectual adventurer. Scientific education is partly responsible, but not wholly. Hudson's point would seem to be that it is the natural convergers who are attracted to the study of science, and the natural divergers who are attracted to the study of the arts and the social sciences. The situation would seem both to answer a need in people and to be self-perpetuating.

On a view like that presented by Hudson, the scientist ought to have something in common with the religious man. They seem to share attitudes of preferring to accept things on authority, of 'commitment', of thinking within limits provided for them. Religion involves respect for tradition: the continuing institution of the Church is of central importance in Christianity. And the religious person is expected to accept the doctrines traditionally laid down: although he may claim latitude to some extent in the interpretation of these doctrines he is not permitted, and does not expect, to invent new doctrines for himself.

We have now two opposed views of the scientific attitude. According to one of them the scientific attitude and the religious attitude are rather different. According to the other they are rather similar. However, there need not be a serious problem of reconciliation; for both views may be true—for example, in the following way. It is not uncommon for there to be a difference between the attitudes and the practices of the leading members of a profession and those of the members who follow them at a distance. It is the difference between originality and conformity. By definition, the original thinkers and practitioners in any field will not be—or not in all respects at any rate—conformists. Equally, by definition, those who are not original will be people who conform in their thinking and practice to what has been laid down by others. The comparison between religion and science probably ought to be made on more than one level. We need to compare the ordinary conventional religious believer with the ordinary conventional scientist, and the prophet, mystic, or religious founder with the great innovating figures in science. Then what we may see is likeness rather than difference. But the likeness may not be so much a likeness between religious attitudes and scientific attitudes as merely an application of a more general likeness between manifestations of originality and manifestations of conformism and conventionality. What makes the ordinary religious believer like the ordinary scientist may have nothing to do with the nature of religion or science, but only with ordinariness. Hudson himself is careful to resist simple invariable equations between divergence (as a personality trait) and creativity or originality in thinking, and between convergence and unoriginality (Hudson, pp. 129, 159ff.); but the evidence of his own work and the evidence from others that he discusses certainly justifies a fair degree of adherence to these equations if 'creativity' is suitably qualified.

Another way of providing a reconciliation may be sought in the view developed by Professor Kuhn, according to which 'normal' science is something carried on by people who are united in the acceptance of a certain 'paradigm' which determines for them the scientific 'puzzles' on which they work and where novelty is neither expected nor offered (textbook science), whereas, on the other hand, 'extraordinary' science is something which belongs to rare periods of crisis in science and shows itself in scientific revolution. Kuhn's distinction is one between stages in the development of science rather than one between different sorts of people—scientific followers and original scientific geniuses (see Pratt, p. 71). Accounts of the history of science generally proceed from one great name to the next—as if the history of science could be evened out into a single steady process towards the ultimate goal of 'the truth' (compare the quotation from Freud above). According to Kuhn, a truer picture would be one of a series of infrequent 'revolutions', interspersed with steady routine working on points of detail, without any ultimate aim or direction. (For Kuhn's views see Kuhn; Lakatos and Musgrave; Pratt.)

What has probably been the most widely accepted view of science in recent years—one associated chiefly with the name of Popper (see Popper, especially the first and third essays)—includes a view about the scientific attitude. It is the view of the scientist as a man who (ideally) never supposes that he has reached finality, never supposes that he has discovered the final truth. For one thing, if there were such a thing as the final truth how could anyone know that he had attained it? Nevertheless, the scientist sees science as a single on-going cooperative enterprise (this is disputed by Kuhn); scientists work upon their own and other scientists' theories, and never rest in the belief that no better theories can be obtained than at present exist. It has been suggested that this attitude provides a bridge between 'the two cultures'. There is as much room for imagination and original thinking in science as in some of the humanities, in particular in the study of literature. There can be no final view on the interpretation of, say, King Lear. There is always room for someone to look at such a work in a new way.

But religion does not seem to offer this kind of scope for imagination and originality in interpretation. That is not to say that new theologies do not appear—such as Tillich's, or that of the Death of God school, or, in earlier centuries, the kind of Protestant modernism or liberalism already referred to which grew up in the last century in response largely to the challenge of science, or Aquinas' creation of a system of theological thought making use of Aristotelian terminology. But it is generally accepted that a proper way of criticising a new theology is by pointing out that it diverges from the traditional way of approaching the problems with which it deals. Admittedly, a new theology can in the course of time come to constitute on its own account an accepted tradition, as in the cases of Aquinas or liberal Protestantism (this might be said to parallel Kuhn's scientific revolutions); but only by coming to be acknowledged as the best interpretation of the fundamental doctrines of Christianity, which are at all times understood to be *given*—in the Bible. Religion has a basis in authority and involves respect for authority, which is importantly different from Popper's understanding of the scientific attitude. We shall pursue these points further in the rest of this chapter, where we turn from the discussion of attitudes to the discussion of methods.

2. *The methods of science and the methods of theology*

It will be better, now that we are to consider methods, to take the contrast as one between science and theology, rather than between science and religion.

According to Popper, the method of science is hypothetico-deductive, or a method of conjecture and refutation. (Kuhn is in dispute with Popper on this point, but we shall suppose that the field of application of the method of conjecture and refutation is limited to Kuhn's 'normal' science. By ignoring its relevance to questions about which of two rival paradigms is to be preferred—that is, by excluding this method from 'extraordinary' science—we may hope to be able to proceed without becoming further involved in at least one important disagreement between Kuhn's view and Popper's. Our concern is, after all, with the philosophy of religion and not with the philosophy of science.) On Popper's view the scientist puts forward a hypothesis—how he arrives at it does not matter—deduces what ought to be the case if the hypothesis is correct, and then attempts to find evidence that will (not support but) falsify it. If it survives his attempts to falsify it, it may be allowed to stand in the meantime; but it is always open to falsification by some scientist in the future. We may add four further points not stressed by Popper but generally accepted as also being part of the methods of science: (1) the scientist's hypotheses are generalisations, i.e. the scientist is interested not in the explanation of particular cases but rather in the explanation of all cases of a certain kind, and particular cases are taken only as examples; (2) the scientist's methods are empirical,

i.e. his speculations are about things that are either in themselves
or in their effects open to sense inspection; (3) the scientist uses
models or analogies in the construction or presentation of hypotheses—certainly in their presentation to a lay audience, but also
for his own professional purposes, either merely as a way of reducing
otherwise intolerably abstract thought to graspable form or, according to some views (e.g. see Hesse), as intrinsic to science and not
merely as a help to scientists; (4) in many sciences (notably physics)
mathematics is an indispensable tool, though there are some sciences
(e.g. geology) where it is much less important for the scientist to be
numerate.

There are some fairly sharp contrasts between the methods of
scientists on the view just described, and those of theologians.
Theology is not a matter of putting forward, for refutation, conjectures arrived at no one knows whence. The subject matter of
theology is a body of doctrine. This is *given*; and although there is
room for conjecture about the interpretation of particular pieces
of doctrine, the doctrines themselves are not held as conjectures or
hypotheses. Even if they were conjectures, the theologian would not
regard himself as having the responsibility of trying to refute them.
Or even if he did, empirical methods would not be likely to strike
him as appropriate. Further, he is interested in the particular case,
as the scientist is not: the theological phrase 'the scandal of particu-
larity', both indicates the theologian's acceptance of the fact that
the notion of the Incarnation presents problems, and in a striking
way calls attention to the fact that he insists upon the particular case.
It may be allowed that theologians, like scientists, use models and
analogies in their thinking (in the theological case, however, the
view that these are merely useful devices could hardly be allowed).
The point about numerateness would seem to be of no great significance either way.

The heart of the matter concerns the contrast between science as
dealing in hypotheses coming no matter whence and theology as
dealing in a body of given doctrine. I remarked above that the period
of warfare between religion and science served to bring about greater
clarity on the question of the different methods of science and theology, and also that at an earlier stage of this developing process of
clarification it seemed to many that the differences were not great:
theology has indeed sometimes been seen as pseudo-science. The
phrase 'the religious hypothesis', which was used by Hume, indicates
an attitude to theology which sees it as attempting to do what science
does—only, he thought, not doing it so well. However, to regard the
theologian as being on all fours with the scientist in putting forward
hypotheses—in particular, the *hypothesis* of the existence of God—

would be to falsify an absolutely central feature of traditional theistic religion: its foundation in doctrines authoritatively provided by the founders of the religion and not in hypotheses dreamed up by imaginative theologians and offered for testing. It might be objected to this that the doctrines which are given to the theologian as his starting point should be seen in relation not to the conjectures of scientists but to the facts ('Nature') which the scientist is trying to explain, and that from this point of view there is a parallel between the attempts of theologians to provide explanations of, or correct formulations of, these doctrines and the scientists' conjectures. I should reply that such a way of putting the matter obscures the extent to which the theologians' basis lies in certain verbal formulae, as the scientists', at the ultimate level, does not. Nevertheless, on the level of interpretation of the basic theological doctrines it may be allowed that there is something that has an affinity with a method of conjecture. We shall consider this more closely in the rest of this section.

We have already, in Chapter 1, in the course of considering the notion of commitment, discussed to some extent the application of Popper's views to theology that has been made by Bartley. It is necessary now to return to this theme, as it bears directly on the question of the relation between the methods of theology and the methods of science. Popper himself makes one reference to religion in his lecture 'On the Sources of Knowledge and of Ignorance'. In writing of the rejection of authority he refers to Kant's ethics and then continues: 'Kant boldly carried this idea into the field of religion: ". . . in whatever way," he writes, "the Deity should be made known to you, and even . . . if He should reveal Himself to you: it is you . . . who must judge whether you are permitted to believe in Him, and to worship Him" ' (Popper, p. 26). This passage from Kant is clearly quoted with approval, but Popper does not enlarge upon it. Bartley's discussion is about theology more than it is about religion.

To proceed by a method of 'conjecture and refutation' would seem to be possible, *up to a point*, in the case of theology. In theology there are what can be called theories, hypotheses, conjectures, and these are improved upon in the course of time as the result of a process of criticism. As Bartley points out (Bartley, p. 63, footnote), Karl Barth uses the words 'essay' and 'hypothesis' of theological statements: theological statements, says Bartley, are therefore *conjectures* about the Word of God, according to Barth, and theology has the critical task of correcting dogma (against the criterion of the Word of God).

There is, then, some relevance of the conjecture-refutation method to theology. At the same time, it is hard to see that theology could get along without appeal to authority. The conjecture-refutation approach fits best the case of science: it only part-fits theology.

Knowledge advances, we are told, by a process in which conjectures are submitted to criticism. But what kind of criticism? Bartley lists four 'means for eliminating error by criticising our conjectures and speculations' (Bartley, pp. 158–9). These are:

(1) The check of *logic*: Is the theory in question consistent?

(2) The check of *sense observation*: Is the theory empirically refutable by some sense observation? And if it is, do we know of any refutation of it?

(3) The check of *scientific theory*: Is the theory, whether or not in conflict with sense observation, in conflict with any scientific hypothesis?

(4) The check of the *problem*: What problem is the theory intended to solve? Does it do so successfully?

The only one of these that Bartley discusses fully is the first— 'the check of logic'. This list of critical methods obviously owes most to science. Even from the point of view of science, however, one of them appears questionable, namely, the third, 'the check of scientific theory'. It is a legitimate criticism of a conjecture, Bartley seems to be saying here, that it is in conflict with 'any' scientific hypothesis. But some conjectures will themselves be scientific hypotheses. This is how science is supposed to advance, by the putting forward of conjectures and having them criticised. But if one of the criticisms is allowed to be that the newer conjectures are in conflict with previous conjectures then how will advance take place? How do you disprove existing scientific hypotheses if one of the methods you are supposed to use assumes them as tests? It would seem to be necessary to be selective in the use of these critical methods. How selective is one allowed to be?

I have pointed out that this list of critical methods seems to owe most to science. If one were thinking in terms of, say, history, let alone of theology, one might want to add to it, or put a particular stress on some part of it. The theologian might want to add 'personal experience', or 'conformity with the teachings of Jesus' to the list. The methods of the historian certainly ought to be relevant to theology; if Christianity is an historical religion, as it is generally said to be, may not checking against sources be an important critical method in Christian theology? To put it roughly: the question to be asked must sometimes be not 'Is this true?' but 'Does this agree with the teachings of Jesus?'

It is difficult to see how widely the four critical methods mentioned do apply to theology. Some theologians say that talk about God cannot be expected to be consistent. How can God be pinned down in some consistent formulation? What is the relevance to theological

theories of the question, 'Is the theory empirically refutable by some
sense observation?' What relevance has this question to, say,
Anselm's theory of the Atonement, or N. P. Williams' theory of a
Cosmic Fall? Again, how far need we ask of a theological theory
whether it is in conflict with any scientific hypothesis? Many such
theories are hardly touched by scientific hypotheses. The final test,
'the test of the problem', it may seem, is bound to be relevant.
Granted that a theory is put forward as a solution to some problem
it can always be asked what problem it is intended to solve and
whether it succeeds in doing so. Nevertheless, problems can be
genuine or otherwise. That there is a problem in the sense that some
question can be formulated to which the theory is supposed to be
an answer does not tell us whether this is a question worth asking,
or whether it does or does not rest on confusion. As for whether
the theory answers the problem successfully, it is notorious that in
practically any branch of study there are opposing schools of thought,
which even when they are agreed on what the problems are, are not
agreed on which theories offer solutions. There are cases where we
cannot ask whether a theory offers a solution—except in a rather
trivial verbal sense—without also asking in whose opinion it offers
a solution.

Whatever may be the situation in science, as far as theology is
concerned the four critical methods do not take us very far. Are we
to say that theology is at fault in not measuring up to these standards?
We should probably need to say the same of ethics; for at least two
of the tests—the check of sense observation and the check of scientific
theory—are equally irrelevant there too. Bartley himself does not
enlarge on the question of what critical methods would be appropriate to inquiries other than scientific ones, and he notes that there
is considerable disagreement about this. I have suggested two
methods in the case of theology: personal experience and conformity
with the teachings of Jesus. If we want to add to these we come up
against the difficulty just mentioned of the existence of opposed
schools of thought in theology. Conformity with the teachings of the
Church Fathers might be a test for one, agreement with the Inner
Light for another; but neither might be happy to use the other's
test.

Naturally, there must be some check on the multiplication of
critical methods. If critical methods are 'means for eliminating error',
we cannot allow just any methods to be adopted. But the method
of appeal to authority (to an authoritative source of knowledge),
though it is not, from Popper's or Bartley's point of view, a means
for eliminating error in science, does seem to serve this purpose in
theology. A large part of Christian theology is the exposition and

explanation of what is claimed to be revealed doctrine; and if theology is to avoid error it must be subject to constant check against the authoritative source of that body of doctrine, whatever that source is taken to be. In this sense the methods of theology are importantly different from the methods of science, and theological (and religious) knowledge is importantly different from scientific knowledge; at any rate on Popper's view of science and scientific knowledge. It may be remarked that theology is by no means so different from (normal) science on Kuhn's view of science as it is on Popper's.

7

GROUNDS FOR BELIEF

1. *Internal and external reasons*

As I have used the terms, the religious sceptic is to be distinguished
from the religious doubter in the following way: belief in any of the
doctrines of religion is incompatible with scepticism about those
doctrines (at any rate, to the extent that the doctrines in question
are doctrines that the believer is committed to; and some element
of commitment is involved in religious belief), whereas belief in any
of the doctrines of religion is not incompatible with the harbouring
of doubts about them. We can be both committed to a belief yet
sometimes doubt it; but we cannot be committed to it yet not
committed to it, or at any rate not in the same respect, and the
sceptic is by definition not committed to religious belief. In fact,
scepticism need not be total: in order to be able to describe someone
as a sceptic it does not seem necessary to require that he should see
no sense or truth in any part whatever of religious belief.

Let us now suppose a debate between a sceptic and a religious
believer about the grounds of religious belief, in the sense not of
the grounds on which some given belief might be held but rather
the grounds on which religious-belief-in-general might be held—
a debate about whether there are good grounds or reasons for being
a religious believer.

Scepticism about alleged grounds of religious belief in this sense
might be met by a believer in at least the following three ways: he
could deny that there are any grounds at all (and thus deny the
relevance of the sceptic's specific criticisms of various suggested
grounds of religious belief); he could claim that there are grounds of
religious belief but that they are grounds that only the believer can
appreciate (so that the sceptic, as an 'outsider', is rejecting what he

does not, and cannot, understand); or, finally, he could agree that there are grounds and that they are open to be grasped and assessed by anyone, whether believer or sceptic, and could then claim that they are good grounds.

The notion of 'grounds' for religious belief is a general one. Religious beliefs, as we have noted earlier, are themselves of different kinds. If there are grounds for religious belief then the empirical element in religious belief presumably has, or lacks, the same sort of grounds as empirical beliefs in other fields. The grounds—if it is appropriate to speak here of grounds—on which the moral element in religion is held are presumably the grounds on which moral beliefs of any kind are held. Or at any rate, some of the grounds on which beliefs of these kinds are held will be the same; for there are, it seems, additional grounds in the case of religious beliefs—in particular, authority: it is appropriate in the case of religion to rest one's belief about (alleged) matters of fact or one's acceptance of certain moral principles on the authority of (for example) Scripture, although to offer authority as an additional ground of such beliefs is not to imply that the beliefs are not to be classed as empirical or as moral beliefs, and it is not to imply that the 'usual' grounds on which empirical or moral beliefs are held are not nevertheless also appropriate.

The first of the three views mentioned maintains that grounds are irrelevant to religious-belief-in-general; but what sort of grounds and why? The question 'Why?' can be answered, for example, in terms of the corruption of man's fallen nature, as by Neo-Protestantism, or in terms of the limitations of speculative reason, as by Kant. The question 'What sort of grounds?' would be answered, certainly by Kant, in terms of the grounds offered by traditional natural theology. But in a sufficiently wide, or at any rate different, sense of 'grounds' neither Kant nor the Neo-Protestants would deny that there are grounds of religious belief; namely, in 'practical reason' or in revelation. There is also a difference between any view which sees in the state of the human mind or soul the condition of there being no grounds (in some qualified sense) of religious belief and any view which concludes to a certain state of the human mind or soul as a consequence of finding suggested grounds logically inadequate. On the latter, far from no useful dialogue being possible between believer and sceptic it is probably as a result of such a dialogue that this position is arrived at. For grounds (of whatever kind, but I am thinking particularly of the traditional theistic 'proofs') to be pronounced irrelevant after they have been found to fail tests is different from their being pronounced irrelevant in the beginning and therefore not tested. Kant seems to hold versions of both these positions. Karl Barth holds the second. The kind of Christian apologist who is castigated by Flew for inconsistency (see Chapter 2, section 4) is probably in some of his moods adopting the first position.

The second view maintained that the sceptic, as an outsider, cannot hope to see as reasons or grounds what the believer sees as reasons or grounds. It is an objection to this that the sceptic, or at any rate the philosophical sceptic, does not reject alleged reasons for religious belief without argument; though, admittedly, the believer might want to say that the sceptic's argued objections to suggested reasons are largely based on misunderstanding. Also, the sceptic is in any case not an outsider to religion, in one important sense at least: he may not share fully the way of life of the believer but in our society a sceptic about religion would find it difficult to avoid exposure to religious influences, and indeed sceptics will commonly be people who are reacting against influences on their own earlier lives. The sceptic has a duty to inform himself as well as he can about religion, a duty not to reject religious beliefs without serious study of what intelligent believers have said about their belief and its grounds. If the sceptic were completely outside religion then presumably it would be the case that nothing he said would really touch religion, except accidentally, and what he said could indeed be ignored by the believer. Yet dialogue does take place; believers and sceptics do not always seem to be addressing themselves to totally different questions. Nevertheless, it seems intuitively correct to say that the sceptic does sometimes miss the point—the believer's point. (There can, of course, be degrees of failure to appreciate another's point of view.) And, certainly, to claim that a certain set of religious beliefs, or a certain religious point of view, can be defended by good reasons does not commit us to saying that everyone will see—or if he sees will acknowledge—that the reasons are good reasons.

If a believer wants to reject some arguments by sceptics against alleged grounds of religious belief, he will be in a stronger position if he maintains that grounds are irrelevant than if he agrees with the sceptic that they are relevant but claims that the sceptic completely fails to understand or appreciate them. Does this latter position mean that the sceptic rejects the grounds for belief (as he rejects religious beliefs themselves) because he does not understand them, and that he does not understand them because he rejects them? (Anselm again: 'unless I believe I shall not understand'.) A more reasonable version of this view would claim that the sceptic does not *fully* understand belief or its grounds, or fails to see their point as the believer sees it, rather than that he fails to see even a glimmering of a point. He half-understands them and rejects what he half-understands. This milder version seems to fit the facts better, for reasons already given, and it avoids one objection to the more extreme version—namely, that if it is maintained that the sceptic cannot understand at all the beliefs of the religious believer, or cannot appreciate at all the reasons the believer might give (because these are reasons purely internal to the religious tradition in question, and the sceptic is entirely excluded from that tradition), then it is arguable that it would be impossible for the sceptic to know that the reasons he is rejecting are the reasons the believer accepts: yet both believer and sceptic would normally want to say that what the one accepts the other rejects.

The identification of belief and understanding has been defended by Professor D. Z. Phillips. Phillips develops an account of Christian love, and puts forward the view that 'to see the possibility of such love amounts to the same thing as coming to see the possibility of belief in God' (Phillips [2], p. 76). He concludes from his discussion that 'there is no theoretical knowledge of God' (p. 79). 'The man who construes religious belief as a theoretical affair distorts it. Kierkegaard emphasises that there is no understanding of religion without passion. That is why understanding religion is incompatible with scepticism' (ibid.). (This last sentence is intended as a denial of the position adopted by Professor Alasdair MacIntyre in an essay entitled 'Is Understanding Religion Compatible with Believing?' (in Hick [1]), which Phillips has just been discussing.) It would seem to be the case that sceptics, in general, lack passion; though some sceptics are perhaps passionately sceptical: and certainly the sceptic does often seem to fail to understand—at any rate understand fully— what the religious believer is wanting to say. Phillips' position would seem to be that the former characteristic of sceptics explains the latter: scepticism is a theoretical attitude, whereas religious understanding involves, or requires, passion.

Phillips maintains that the enterprise of seeking a justification of religious belief in terms of reasons external to the religion itself is fundamentally mistaken. 'The whole conception . . . of religion standing in need of justification [that is, by tests taken from some other context] is confused' (Phillips [1], p. 10). The criteria for truth in religion are to be found *within* religious traditions themselves (see ibid., p. 27). Phillips writes as follows of 'one class of' reasons for religious belief:

Religious believers, when asked why they believe in God, may reply in a variety of ways. They may say, 'I have had an experience of the living God', 'I believe on the Lord Jesus Christ', 'God saved me while I was a sinner', or, 'I just can't help believing'. Philosophers have not given such reasons very much attention. The so-called trouble is not so much with the content of the replies, as with the fact that the replies are made by believers. The answers come from *within* religion, they presuppose the framework of Faith, and therefore cannot be treated as *evidence* for religious belief (Phillips [2], p. 63).

Phillips is undoubtedly right in saying that reasons given by religious believers themselves ought not to be rejected by philosophers *for that reason*. But religious believers are of different kinds. It is true that many believers might want to reply to the question why they believe in God in the terms just mentioned. But some have wanted to reply in other terms—including the traditional theistic proofs. The theistic proofs of traditional natural theology might be classed either as reasons external to, or as reasons internal to, religion, depending on circumstances. At any rate, one or other of the traditional theistic proofs has seemed to offer a reason for believing in God to some who were believers, for example, as we saw earlier, Paley (that is, reasons in further support of already-held beliefs). Phillips is suggesting that philosophers do not give much attention to those reasons for belief that are offered by believers themselves or that presuppose the framework of Faith. But *all* reasons for belief have been offered by believers —one could hardly imagine them occurring to anyone else—and all of them are likely on some occasions of their use to have been used in such a way that they presuppose 'the framework of Faith' (compare Paley's remarks about his use of the Argument from Design, or my comments in Chapter 4, section 2, on the Cosmological Argument). It is conceivable that an enemy of religion might devise and make public a bad argument ostensibly in support of religious belief merely in order to be able then to refute that argument. But this seems unlikely, and in any case we are invited to consider only reasons that might be given by believers; and if a believer accepted such a Trojan horse of an argument at its face value and himself spread it abroad it would then become, whatever its origins, just one more reason that religious believers have given for religious belief. It cannot be the fact that they are offered by believers that leads many philosophers, as Phillips says, to ignore reasons like those he mentions; for if this were so, one would expect them to ignore the traditional theistic proofs, instead of, as some do, devoting a fair amount of attention to them. Nor can it be because they presuppose the framework of Faith, for this is true of the theistic proofs on some understandings of them. Is it because the believers' reasons he instances are not *arguments*? But the first of them at least is capable of being developed into an argument, and frequently is. I would suggest that philosophers neglect such reasons as those mentioned by Phillips principally because they seem to them to be weak reasons; in other words, that it *is*, despite what Phillips says, the content of the reasons that leads to their being ignored.

There is some ambiguity in the notion of accepting or rejecting something as a reason. To say that a philosopher ignores some reasons for belief that are offered by believers might mean that to that philosopher they do not look like reasons at all, that they do not begin to be the sort of thing that would qualify as reasons. Or it might mean that the philosopher, although he would be prepared to acknowledge that they qualify as reasons of a kind, rejects them as bad or insufficient reasons. Phillips certainly considers that the philosopher has no right to pronounce upon the goodness or badness of the reasons offered by believers. But in order for a philosopher to be able to refrain from pronouncing upon the goodness or badness of alleged reasons it is necessary for him at least to acknowledge that they are the kind of thing that can be allowed to be reasons, however good or bad. Otherwise, what is he refraining from? And it is hard to see how he could be said meaningfully to acknowledge that something was the sort of thing that might be allowed to be a reason unless he, to some extent, understood it. And unless his understanding of it in some way agrees with the believer's understanding of it there would be no point in saying that he is refraining from passing judgement on that very reason that the believer is offering.

Phillips, if I understand him, allows that there is nothing to preclude a philosopher from accepting that from the point of view of a believer such-and-such a thing might be given as a reason for religious belief; the philosopher can certainly try to enter into a way of life that is foreign to him and may succeed to some extent in seeing matters from the point of view of those who belong to that way of life. The point I am making, however, is a stronger one—namely, that some understanding of the believer's way of life (some entering into that way of life) on the part of the (possibly sceptical) philosopher is *entailed* by Phillips' belief that the philosopher has no right to pronounce upon the religious believers' reasons for belief. The philosopher cannot recognise them as alleged reasons for belief without understanding them to some degree. Equally the philosopher cannot reject such alleged reasons without understanding them to some degree. Yet we are told that understanding religion is incompatible with scepticism. If belief requires understanding, so does scepticism. Phillips does not defend the position that the form of life of the believer is *totally* closed to the understanding of outsiders (see Phillips [3]), but there is some element of reluctance in his concessions. It would seem, however, that he is bound to acknowledge that understanding does not preclude scepticism.

2. *Hypotheses and affirmations*

We may here consider another question that concerns the enterprise of seeking grounds for religious belief. It is said that such an enterprise makes the mistake of interpreting religious beliefs as hypotheses (if they were hypotheses it would certainly be in order to seek for evidence in support of them or reasons for holding them), whereas they are properly to be seen as commitments in faith or affirmations of trust (and it is inappropriate to seek for evidence in support of such commitments or affirmations). For example, Professor J. Kellenberger has argued against Flew's 'falsification challenge' (as he calls it) that Flew is treating religious utterances as hypotheses when he asks what would have to happen to convince someone that he was no longer justified in saying 'God loves us' (see Kellenberger; also McPherson [2]). Now it is important to see that although it is undoubtedly true that the believer makes affirmations of trust and does not hold his religious beliefs, or at any rate the more important of them, in the manner of hypotheses, this does not of itself preclude an examination of the content of the beliefs and the grounds (if any) for holding them. The fact that a man is *committed to* a set of beliefs does not render him immune from questions, posed either by others or by himself, about what those beliefs mean and on what evidence or other grounds they may be held. It is true that the more firmly he is committed the less likely he may be in practice to consider such questions; but they may be important questions. Probably, indeed, the more firmly a man is committed to a belief the more necessary, for the sake of his own intellectual development, it is for him sometimes to re-examine the grounds on which he holds it; and when the belief in question is a moral, political or religious one, it may be of practical importance for others that he should sometimes re-examine it. A man might be committed to a set of absurd or wicked beliefs. The mere fact that he was committed to them would not mean that it was inappropriate to ask him to explain them and defend them. He would be within his rights in refusing; but we might still, for practical or moral reasons, think it important to press him.

To describe beliefs as commitments is elliptical. Commitment— or affirmation of trust, etc.—is not a kind of belief so much as an attitude towards belief. What we commit ourselves *to*, where this is a propositional belief or set of propositional beliefs, can be expressed as an assertion or set of assertions, and questions about grounds can generally be raised. To describe a belief as a commitment or an affirmation of trust, or something of the sort, does not of itself preclude the raising of questions about the grounds of that belief. The same proposition cannot at one and the same time by one and the

I

same person be *held* both tentatively and firmly; but the question of the degree of firmness with which a belief is held is not the same as the question of the logical status of what is held. I can hold with the utmost firmness that the earth is round: however, this does not mean either that I hold this 'irrationally' (there is no necessary connection between being committed to a belief and being unable to give reasons for it: see the discussion in Chapter 1, section 4, and elsewhere in the book), or that the belief about the earth that I hold so firmly cannot itself be described as an hypothesis, supportable, and as it happens extremely well supported, by evidence. Professor Basil Mitchell writes:

There are certain questions which in practice a man has to decide, or to live as if he had decided. They are no longer open questions for him, though they may once have been and may conceivably become so again. His attitude to them may thus vary, but this variation in his attitude does not affect their logical status. They may be, from a logical point of view, hypotheses, based on evidence and liable to be confirmed or refuted by further evidence; but so long as he is trying to live by them he does not, and cannot, treat them as hypotheses. They may become for him ultimate and fundamental convictions, which determine his priorities and decisively shape his attitudes and interests, and help to make him the sort of man that he is; but this does not dictate an answer to the question whether or to what extent they can be justified. It certainly does not imply that no question of justification can arise. A man does not contradict himself if he is prepared to give reasons why, ultimately, he is a Christian or a Marxist (Mitchell [2]; High, p. 186).

Some half-believers become believers, and some believers cease to believe. This can be by some kind of rational process, though, of course, it is often a non-rational matter. There may well not be knock-down arguments, in favour of, or against, religious belief; and there seems to be a certain inappropriateness about the notion that there might be. But there are considerations tending to the support of religious belief. A theory of religious belief ought not to concentrate only on the nature of religious belief at the expense of a consideration of how people come to be believers or how they would defend their belief if it were challenged. Religious practices—of prayer, etc.—may help to confirm people in religious belief, but so may reflection on the theistic 'proofs'. Some 'reasons for belief' become stronger, others become weaker, as reflection and religious practice go on. Certainly people's religious condition changes, and their faith waxes and wanes.

It is now appropriate to return to the main line of argument of the chapter and take up briefly the third of the original three views. The believer may claim that there are indeed grounds for religious belief, and that these are open to be understood and assessed by sceptics as well as believers. Our discussion of the second view has itself led on to the third; I have tried to show that this third view is, as has indeed traditionally been supposed, a possible and proper view. At the same time, we need to carry over into this third view the qualification that the sceptic is unlikely to be able to appreciate either belief or the grounds for belief quite as the believer does; this would seem to be no more than an acknowledgement of plain fact.

It is not illegitimate for the believer both to acknowledge that a sceptic can understand and assess reasons for religious belief but nevertheless sometimes counter particular criciticisms offered by the sceptic by saying, 'But you don't really understand'. The believer would not be inconsistent even if he acknowledged that sceptics can understand and assess reasons and yet *always* rejected a particular sceptic's criticisms as being based on failure to understand; for he might with justice be able to say that that sceptic had not tried nearly hard enough to see the point of the beliefs or their reasons. But, of course, the believer would have to go warily in using that kind of defence; for there must be a real danger of falling into a fault parallel to that pointed out by Flew in 'Theology and Falsification'.

What then *are* the grounds of religious belief? I do not propose to attempt an answer to that question. I shall make two points only. First, the grounds may be very various, and not every believer will answer the question in the same way. My concern in this chapter has been mainly to suggest that (some) such grounds may be assess-able by both believer and non-believer. An account of the grounds of religious belief is likely to extend as widely as an account of religious belief itself. Secondly, it is important to remember, as has been remarked more than once already, that there is no obligation upon religious believers to articulate in propositions the grounds of their belief either to themselves or to others—though sometimes there might be a strong pressure on them to do so, from themselves or from others. The topic is then, although a proper one, also an avoidable one, both for the believer and the philosopher.

BIBLIOGRAPHY

St Anselm, *Proslogion:* trans. in S. N. Deane, *St Anselm: Proslogium; Monologium; an Appendix in Behalf of the Fool by Gaunilon*; and *Cur Deus Homo* (Chicago 1930). Translation of Chs. II–IV, and of Gaunilo's criticisms and Anselm's reply, in Hick and McGill (q.v.).

St Thomas Aquinas, *Summa Theologica*, trans. Fathers of the English Dominican Province (London 1920–8). For the Five Ways see vol. 1.

A. J. Ayer, *Language, Truth and Logic* (2nd ed., London 1946).

W. W. Bartley, *The Retreat to Commitment* (London 1964).

R. B. Braithwaite, *An Empiricist's View of the Nature of Religious Belief* (Cambridge 1955); reprinted in Mitchell [3], to which page references are given.

F. C. Copleston, *Aquinas* (Harmondsworth 1955).

Michael Durrant [1], 'St Thomas's "Third Way"', in *Religious Studies* **4** (1968).

Michael Durrant [2], *Theology and Intelligibility* (London 1973).

Antony Flew, *Hume's Philosophy of Belief* (London 1961).

Antony Flew and Alasdair MacIntyre, Eds., *New Essays in Philosophical Theology* (London 1955).

Sigmund Freud, *The Future of an Illusion*, trans. W. D. Robson-Scott (London 1949).

P. T. Geach, *God and the Soul* (London 1969).

Stuart Hampshire, *Thought and Action* (London 1959).

R. S. Heimbeck, *Theology and Meaning* (London 1969).

Mary B. Hesse, *Models and Analogies in Science* (London 1963).

John Hick [1], Ed., *Faith and the Philosophers* (London 1964).

John Hick [2], *Evil and the God of Love* (London 1966).

John Hick and Arthur McGill, Eds., *The Many-Faced Argument* (London 1968).

Dallas M. High, *New Essays on Religious Language* (New York 1969).

Liam Hudson, *The Contrary Imagination* (Harmondsworth 1967).

David Hume [1], *Enquiries concerning the Human Understanding and concerning the Principles of Morals*, Ed. L. A. Selby-Bigge, (2nd ed. Oxford 1966).

David Hume [2], *Dialogues concerning Natural Religion*, Ed. N. Kemp Smith (2nd ed., London 1947).

Robert H. Hurlbutt, *Hume, Newton, and the Design Argument* (Lincoln, Nebraska 1965).

Immanuel Kant, *Critique of Pure Reason*, trans. N. Kemp Smith (London 1968).
J. Kellenberger, 'The Falsification Challenge', in *Religious Studies* **5** (1969); reprinted in Kellenberger's *Religious Discovery, Faith, and Knowledge* (Englewood Cliffs, New Jersey 1972).
Anthony Kenny, *The Five Ways* (London 1969).
K. E. Kirk, *Some Principles of Moral Theology and their Application* (London 1920).
S. Körner, *Kant* (Harmondsworth 1955).
Thomas S. Kuhn, *The Structure of Scientific Revolutions* (2nd ed., Chicago 1970).
Imre Lakatos and Alan Musgrave, Eds., *Criticism and the Growth of Knowledge* (Cambridge 1970).
G. W. von Leibniz, *Theodicy, Essays on the Goodness of God, the Freedom of Man and the Origin of Evil*, trans. E. M. Huggard, Ed. Austin Farrer (London 1952).
H. D. Lewis, *Our Experience of God* (London 1959).
John Locke, *The Second Treatise of Civil Government* and *A Letter concerning Toleration*, Ed. J. W. Gough (Oxford 1946).
J. L. Mackie, 'Evil and Omnipotence', in *Mind* **64** (1955); reprinted in Mitchell [3] and in Pike (q.v.).
E. L. Mascall, *Existence and Analogy* (London 1949).
Thomas McPherson [1], *The Philosophy of Religion* (London 1965).
Thomas McPherson [2], 'The Falsification Challenge: A Comment', in *Religious Studies* **5** (1969).
Thomas McPherson [3], *The Argument from Design* (London 1972).
Basil Mitchell [1], Ed., *Faith and Logic* (London 1957).
Basil Mitchell [2], 'The Justification of Religious Belief', in *The Philosophical Quarterly* **11** (1961); reprinted in High (q.v.).
Basil Mitchell [3], Ed., *The Philosophy of Religion* (London 1971).
R. C. Mortimer, *The Elements of Moral Theology* (rev. ed., London 1953).
Rodney Needham, *Belief, Language, and Experience* (Oxford 1972).
Rudolf Otto, *The Idea of the Holy*, trans. J. W. Harvey (London 1950).
W. Paley, *Natural Theology*, in vol. III of *The Complete Works of William Paley, D. D.* (London 1825).
T. Penelhum, *Religion and Rationality* (New York 1971).
D. Z. Phillips [1], *The Concept of Prayer* (London 1965).
D. Z. Phillips [2], Ed., *Religion and Understanding* (Oxford 1967).
D. Z. Phillips [3], 'Religious Beliefs and Language-Games', in *Ratio* **12** (1970); reprinted in Mitchell [3] (q.v.).
Nelson Pike, Ed., *God and Evil* (Englewood Cliffs, New Jersey 1964).
A. Plantinga, *God and Other Minds* (Ithaca, New York 1967).
K. R. Popper, *Conjectures and Refutations* (3rd ed., London 1969).
Vernon Pratt, review of I. Lakatos and A. Musgrave, Eds., *Criticism and the Growth of Knowledge*, in *Theoria to Theory* **6** (1972).
H. H. Price, *Belief* (London 1969).
Gilbert Ryle, *The Concept of Mind* (London 1949).
Ninian Smart, *A Dialogue of Religions* (London 1960).
R. G. Swinburne, 'The Argument from Design', in *Philosophy* **43** (1968).
C. C. J. Webb, *Kant's Philosophy of Religion* (Oxford 1926).
Bernard Williams and Alan Montefiore, Eds., *British Analytical Philosophy* (London 1966).

INDEX

INDEX